# Stories Jesus Still Tells

# The Parables

# Stories Jesus Still Tells
# The Parables

### John R. Claypool

**MCCRACKEN PRESS**
New York

**McCracken Press™**
**An imprint of Multi Media Communicators, Inc.**
575 Madison Avenue, Suite 1006
New York, NY 10022

McCracken Press™ is a trademark of Multi Media
Communicators, Inc.

Cover by Tim Ladwig

Library of Congress Catalog Card Number:  93-078993

ISBN 1-56977-550-8

10 9 8 7 6 5 4 3 2 1

First Edition

Printed in the United States of America

# Contents

# Introduction

In the long, quiet years of growing up in Nazareth, Jesus was given the task of reconciling the world back to a true understanding of the divine nature.

This wasn't going to be easy; centuries before, the earliest humans had let fear take root in the deepest places in their hearts, and that wreaked havoc with everything. For reasons that will never be clear, our forebears listened to a serpent's word that the Creator wasn't essentially good, that instead he was a vicious exploiter.

Once this image of mistrust possessed their minds and hearts, humans became little more than terrified beasts. They saw threats everywhere, and proceeded to unmake the lovely creation that had come from the divine hand.

Jesus, therefore, faced a major challenge. For centuries, his human brothers and sisters had operated out of a totally false perception of God, a perception that threatened to destroy God's dream of sharing his joy with the creatures of his affection. How could His light be shed on this dark, suspicious place in man's soul?

As Jesus pondered this challenge, a strategy from the Old Testament heritage commended itself to him: the way the prophet Nathan had handled a crisis highly charged with panic and fear. Jesus recalled the story:

King David had reached the pinnacle of military and political power. In four short decades, he had risen from the obscurity of tending his father's sheep to being recognized as the most powerful figure in the whole Mediterranean Basin. From the Nile to the Euphrates, David had no equal. But at this moment of unprecedented professional success, parts of his self, which he had neglected in his headlong climb to fame, broke to the surface and created a personal crisis. Today we call such episodes a mid-life crisis, a time when the imbalances in the way one has lived needed to be addressed.

In David's case, he had obviously given little effort to his own needs for intimacy. As a result, when he was pacing restlessly one afternoon on the roof of his palace—having conquered the world politically, but not having fed the hungers of his own love-starved heart—he saw a beautiful woman bathing... and suddenly he wanted her more than anything else in the world. His great success in one area failed to satisfy the other. David clumsily set about to operate in the realm of love the way he had waged war. He had the woman brought to him by force, and before the night was done, he had raped another man's wife and conceived a child with her.

It's pathetic, really, to look back and see how ill-prepared David was for human relations. When he learned of the woman's pregnancy, he panicked and set in motion a major cover-up. Learning that the woman was the wife of one of his soldiers; he proceeded to manipulate regulations to send the soldier home so it would appear the child was his. When this didn't work, David had the husband sent back to the front to be killed. Then David took the beleaguered woman and made her his wife before the baby was born. This sordid drama took its toll on David. He was frenzied by fevered guilt and panic.

Obviously, God wasn't at all pleased with this episode. Yet remember, David was beloved of God, "a man," the Scripture says, "after God's own heart." The Holy One refused to leave David out on a limb, so to speak. He inspired the prophet Nathan to go to David as a reconciler—just as later God would send Jesus on a similar mission to the world. And, as always, God gave Nathan a way to accomplish this delicate task. (The Holy One never sends one out to struggle on his own—he provides both the means and the end!)

Nathan knew that to confront a frightened person directly might make matters worse. So, Nathan went to David and said, "Let me tell you a story. I want your honest opinion on something." Then he went on to tell him about a rich man who owned vast properties and his a poor tenant, whose sole possession was a single ewe lamb that was treated as if it were a child. One day company arrived unexpectedly at the rich man's house, and instead of sending for one of his many lambs or calves, he took the tenant's lamb, had it butchered, and served for lunch. "How do you evaluate such an action?" asked Nathan.

The king was interested in the story. "That rich man had no sense of justice. What he did was patently unfair. If this case were brought before me, I would pronounce him guilty and demand he repay fourfold for what he unlawfully took."

David might have thought he had rendered a final verdict, but Nathan said quietly, "David, this story is about you and what you did to Bathsheba and Uriah the Hittite." It had worked! The story, a vehicle to get behind David's defenses, enabled him to embrace the sordid truth about himself. That story marked the beginning of a whole new chapter in David's growth.

As Jesus pondered the task given to Him by God, Nathan's use of a story seemed an exceptionally effective way of doing what needed to be done. Under the inspiration of his Father in Heaven, Jesus went on to perfect this methodology as no one has since. He called the stories *parables*, and they became the most distinctive form of his teaching. What the proverb was to Solomon and the fable to Aesop, these special kinds of stories were to Jesus in his mission of reconciliation.

There are certain distinctive features of this particular genre of literature.

*First, the images that Jesus used in weaving these stories were always familiar and drawn from everyday life.* Oftentimes modern writers make allusions that are difficult to understand. Jesus never did that. Even the most illiterate adult could identify with the situations, objects, and persons that he chose as the raw material for his parables.

*Second, these stories were characterized by intriguing plots.* They had a way of drawing people into the movement of the stories, which served the important purpose of lowering defenses and opening breakthroughs of insight.

*Third, perhaps the most distinctive characteristic of the parables is the element of surprise.* When people thought a parable was about someone else, it turned out to be about them! Parables start out as portraits of other people, and then suddenly turn into mirrors in which people see things about themselves that they had not seen before. David found himself looking at a reflection of his own life when Nathan's parable came to its climax.

This is how Jesus worked the miracle of reconciliation again and again. People would come to him in all degrees of panic, fear, and anger. Yet, instead of confronting them head-on and driving them deeper into their defensiveness, he would, like Nathan, defuse their anxiety by saying "Let me tell you a story...." Then, well into the story, with their defenses down, the listeners would see the story as a mirror, and its light would make their personal darkness visible.

In this way, parables became events of revelation. Profound things would happen to people at the deepest levels of their beings and the age-old problem of fear casting out love was reversed. Here was the phenomenon of *love casting out fear,* as human beings saw, as if for the first time, a smile on the face of their Creator/Redeemer. Primal trust was once again restored.

The title of this book could well have been *Nathan's Legacy.* It links the methodology Jesus used with a wisdom that goes far back into Hebrew memory, yet remains a wisdom that is as current as this morning's newspaper. These story-events called *parables* have the same power to reveal us to ourselves and to show us the Father/Mother/Parent God as they did when Jesus first told them.

I invite you to open up the deep places in your being so that "the Light that enlightens up every person" can illumine you as well!

Stories Jesus Still Tells

The Parables

# 1

## The Treasure, The Pearl, and the Dragnet

### Matthew 13:44-50

Ours is a many-splendored universe, or to use the Chinese metaphor, a world of ten thousand things. This means, quite practically, that we're faced with a myriad of options in every direction and that we're called upon to make value judgments at every turn. Carlyle Marney used to say that there was no agony in life more acute than those moments when you realize you've paid too much. It's at these times that you look at what you have, and consider all the sacrifices that went into the procurement of these things, and then sense the disparity between the two. It's at this point that a profound sense of disappointment may settle in. I'd be amazed if there's any adult who is a total stranger to such an experience.

We've no more fundamental task in life than facing up to the fact that there are millions of options laid out before us in a lifetime and that we must decide what is worth what. On the one hand, we can pay too much and confuse something that has only relative value with something that is of absolute value. On the other hand, we can succeed in this endeavor and not only recognize the real and the good and the truly valuable but also organize our lives around such discernments. To that latter end, I am convinced Jesus told these three tiny parables.

—

*The kingdom of Heaven is like a treasure hidden in a field, which a man found and covered up. And then in his joy, he goes and sells all that he has and buys that field. Again the kingdom of Heaven is like a merchant in search of fine pearls who, on finding one pearl of great value, went and sold all that he had and bought it. Again the kingdom of Heaven is like a net which is thrown into the sea to gather fish of every kind. When it was full, the men drew it ashore, sat down and sorted out the good into vessels, but threw away the bad. So it will be at the close of the age. The angels will come and separate the evil from the righteous and throw them into the furnace of fire, and there men shall weep and gnash their teeth.*

—

Jesus utilized images familiar to his hearers. He wasn't an elitist reserving his meanings for the privileged few. There wasn't a peasant of that day who would have had trouble understanding what he was alluding to here.

The first of Jesus's images, discovering buried treasure, wasn't all that unusual. Many a farmer had had the experience of plowing along and suddenly hitting something, only to discover a chest full of coins or jewels or some kind of precious material. For centuries the little nation we know today as Israel had been the battleground across which the two great cultures of the ancient world had fought—the Egyptians and the Babylonians. It was that little bridge of land located between these two superpowers which, again and again, first one and then the other had swept across.

People who had to live through such foreign invasions soon learned that the earth was the only safe place to protect their possessions. By burying things of value, it was harder for these marauding hordes to get their hands on them. For this reason, Israel became pocketed with stashes of treasure, put there when the word got out that some foreign army was approaching. Of course, many times the folk who did this were killed themselves, so their treasures remained in the earth, only to be discovered accidentally by somebody else. Many of Jesus's listeners had undoubtedly had such an experience or known of someone who happened upon a trove in this way.

I now have in my possession just such a family treasure. It consists of eight silver spoons, which in and of themselves have very little value. Like all family heirlooms, however, it's the story behind them that makes them so significant to me. Back in 1862, my great-grandmother on my mother's side was living on a large plantation near Ripley, Mississippi. The Civil War was in full swing. The story is that my forebear looked out of her upstairs window one day and in the distance saw the Union Army coming.

She ran down to the dining room, filled her apron with as much silverware as she could carry, went out in the side yard, dug a shallow hole, put the silverware in it, and then turned an old wash pot over it so the Yankees couldn't see a place so freshly dug up. As it turned out, that silverware was about the only thing that was saved after the invaders got through their plundering. A part of that buried treasure came down to my grandmother and mother and now me, and I shall always cherish it.

The second of Jesus's images is the particular jewel whose value stood above all others in the first century. Diamonds had been discovered by this time, but they were so rare that they played no part in Mediterranean culture. It is the pearl that was regarded as preeminent. Cleopatra, the Queen of the Nile, allegedly had two—one given to her by a suitor, and another supposedly worth about three million dollars in today's currency. The origin of this particular jewel was different than that of other precious stones. A pearl develops when a grain of sand somehow gets inside the shell of an oyster, and cuts the tender membrane to the quick. In reaction to this intrusion, the little organism secretes a milky-like substance to soften the sharp edges, and this takes shape around the particle of sand. In due course, someone comes along and finds the shell, opens it up, and there gleams a lovely pearl as a monument to this process of pain.

Not surprisingly, then, the ancient world valued

pearls as a symbol of hope, of how bad things none-theless give birth to surprisingly good things. That imagery wasn't lost on the biblical writers. If you look carefully at the last book of the Bible—the Revelation of St. John—you will find a symbolic description of the ultimate goal of all history, which is called Heaven. John says the gates into this reality will be formed by this particular jewel, the well-known "pearly gates." And why is that? The symbolism is profound. We are reminded, as we enter the realm of ultimate fulfillment, that we do so because of the creative suffering of a God who cared about us and a Christ who came to die on our behalf. "He was wounded for our transgressions, He was bruised for our iniquities; upon Him was the chas-tisements that made us whole, and with His stripes we are healed" (Isaiah 53:5).

In Jesus's story, a tradesman, perhaps a veteran of many caravan journeys, came across the most exquisite pearl of them all, the loveliest he had ever seen, and responded accordingly. His eye was trained to recog-nize value when he saw it, and this stone prompted decisive action.

The third of Jesus's images grew out of the work of fishermen, a vocation Jesus knew quite well, for he grew up near the Sea of Galilee. These folk would set out in two boats, and when they reached the cen-ter of the lake, let down a large net between them and pull it toward the shore. When the water got shallow enough, they would get out and drag the huge net toward the shore. Then they'd sit down on the bank and sort out the fish. Only those that were edible could be sold; the rest were tossed back into the water.

Basic to all three of these stories, then, is the task of discerning what is worth what. How can we avoid paying too much for things and find the true *summum bonum,* the value of all values, the highest value of all?

Kyle Hazelton has written a little book called *Flux and Fidelity;* in it he makes the point that though human beings have differed widely across the ages, there are two basic drives that remain constant and in every one of us. One is the drive toward self-preservation—people who are healthy want to live on. The other is the yearning to fulfill ourselves—to recognize our potential and to actualize this. And in the service of these two goals, nothing is more crucial than discerning the relative values of all we encounter. When this happens authentically—if I may apply this to what Jesus was saying in these short parables—it has a way of reorganizing all of life and giving birth to new configurations of meaning.

This is certainly the implication of the first two parables. After the farmer encountered the buried treasure and the merchant the unique pearl, their lives became genuinely different. All things were seen in a new light and there was a joyful rearrangement of things. Suddenly there was a willingness to let go of what one did have in order to get something that was obviously better. In other words, when the summum bonum comes along, and is recognized, it changes the way we evaluate everything and can lead to the radical reordering of our lives. It seems clear to me that Jesus was addressing here the whole issue of change and how it occurred in positive and creative ways.

If you stop and think about it, every experience of this sort has two very different sides. On the one hand, we get something that we didn't have, and on the other hand, we give up something that we did have. It wouldn't be change if we didn't gain something and at the same time lose something. At the most basic level, this is what change is and does. In these first two parables, Jesus is saying that healthy change occurs when we discern that the thing that is being offered is greater and better than the thing that is being taken away. This is why he says the man who found the treasure went and sold everything he owned to buy the field, and that he did it with great joy!

This is a very natural process. Creative changes occur in our lives when we discern that what is being given is really of a greater value that what is being asked of us. The same experience, however, becomes destructive when the gain dimension isn't obvious and when all we can think about is the loss dimension. To this way of looking at things, change is by no means a life-enhancing and life-enriching process, but rather a diminishment and a lessening of the good.

I'll never forget how, not long after the death of my daughter, a wise old man said to me, "There's a relief dimension in every experience of grief." To be honest, I couldn't hear his meaning at the time. I was so overwhelmed by my own loss that I was offended at the suggestion that there could be a gain dimension in all this. As I lived on, however, I eventually came to see his point: in every change experience, we're being given something we didn't have before. For example, I did have more time and energy to invest in my living son after his sister died, as well as more money to use for his education. This isn't to say that such a rearrangement is what I'd have chosen, but once the change was thrust upon me, I did have a choice. The point is that the experience of change gives us something as well as takes something away. If we can learn to focus on that side of things, then our attitude toward change can become genuinely different. Instead of digging in our heels and saying, "Come weal, come woe, my status is quo," we can begin to search through all the new things for the gift we're being given.

In the first two parables, the greater value of the new wasn't hard to see. The selling of all to buy what had suddenly become so valuable was hardly a sacrifice. Neither the farmer nor the pearl merchant had to struggle at all, because what they were going to gain became so obvious. I, however, want to go a step further now and say that when the loss dimension seems to be enormous, I believe one can count on the fact that God has seen to it there's something there that can still enhance one's life.

This conviction grows out of the trauma to which I've already referred; namely, the death of my only daughter in 1970. Losing her was painful in every sense of the term, but it wasn't an event of total destructiveness. My own awareness of life as a gift emerged from the agony of that bereavement, and led me to the conviction that in all experiences of change, there's something of value being given. For this reason, we don't have to despair when the landscape of our life is radically altered. There's always a basis for hope, and this leads us to begin to search anew for the blessings that may be hidden in the event.

Both the farmer and the merchant underwent an experience of genuine change, and in both cases the reorganization of life resulted in something even better than they had known. Thus, Jesus invites us to process all changes, not just some changes, hopefully and expectantly.

But this is by no means all that these parables are meant to teach us. I see Jesus returning here to a theme that recurred throughout all his teachings; namely, an emphasis on the first commandment to Moses: "I am the Lord your God, who delivered you out of the land of Egypt. You shall have no other Gods before Me" (Exodus 20:2-3). What is the *summum bonum,* the value above all other values? Jesus called it "the kingdom of Heaven," a term used inter-

changeably with "the Kingdom of God." Exactly
what is this reality? It is God himself and his kingly
rule of all reality.

In the biblical understanding of reality, there are
only two forms—the uncreated and the created.
Nothing but God belongs on the uncreated side of
the line and everything except God belongs on the
created side. This means that we must not expect
something that derives its life from God to be able to
meet all of our needs. Only the very Fountain of all
being possesses that sort of power. Augustine of
Hippo realized this fact well when he wrote, "Thou
hast made us for thyself, O God, and our hearts are
restless until they rest in thee." We are, therefore, to
relate to God as we relate to nothing else, and look to
the Holy One for the secret of our fulfillment. The
kingly rule of God consists in receiving all things
from this One as a gracious gift, and then offering all
things back thankfully and with the prayer, How
should all of this be used? The gifts are then given
back a second time with the added blessing of the
Holy Spirit, who imparts the wisdom we need to use
the gifts of God appropriately.

Thus, "this kingly rule" is to the discerning heart
exactly what the buried treasure was to the one who
discovered it in the field, what the exquisite pearl was
to the true connoisseur of jewels, and what the fish
worth keeping were to the fishermen. Only in allegiance to God can the promise of fulfillment be realized. Ultimate attachment to anything else is called

idolatry, and that is always a recipe for disappointment. Without exception, you'll wind up paying too much when you put ultimate trust in that which is not God, but in one of God's creations.

How do we discern our way into recognition of what is and what isn't of final worth? History suggests that most of us do it by trial and error, seeking first this and then that in an attempt to satisfy the hunger of our hearts. Years ago, when I was doing some work in continuing education, I came across an old book entitled *On Loving God* by Bernard of Clairvaux, one of the foremost reformers of medieval monasticism. Bernard had observed the spiritual development of literally hundreds of monks, and out of all this exposure to folk who were intent on discovering the summum bonum, he came up with a fourfold continuum of successive stages toward real fulfillment. I've found this to be very helpful in understanding what Jesus was talking about in these parables.

Bernard describes stage one as "the love of self for self's sake," the infantile position that is bounded north, south, east, and west by a concern for self and self alone. This is where all of us begin the human journey. We're aware of our needs, and nothing else. The psychological term for this is "narcissism" or "egocentricity," and it does not begin to fully satisfy all the needs of the human psyche.

C. S. Lewis spoke once of being awakened in the middle of the night during his bachelor days and not being able to go back to sleep. It was totally dark and utterly still in his bedroom at Magdalen College. There was no way to perceive anything there outside himself. It was as if he were alone in a vacuous black hole. Suddenly he sat bolt upright in bed, for it dawned on him that such isolation was the logical end of a self-centered life.

"What if," he found himself asking, "we get in eternity exactly what we've lived for in time?" This means if we've truly loved others and beauty and ideas and causes beyond ourselves, we shall continue to participate in that realm of richness. But if we've lived only for ourselves—if every thought and concern have revolved around the self and the self alone—could it be that all we shall get will be ourselves and nothing else?

Such a condition would amount to total isolation, which is similar to that worst of all punishments, short of capital punishment—namely, solitary confinement. Such a fate cuts across the very heart of what we human beings are and need. To be utterly and totally alone makes even the images of a burning Hell seem mild in comparison. We've no choice about beginning our lives in such self-centeredness, but we do have a choice as to whether or not we remain there. Woe be to the person who ends up in the same condition of self-absorption that characterizes our birth. Mercifully, most folk choose to grow.

The second stage is what Bernard called "the love of God for self's sake." Notice now that an awareness of outside realities has been born. There are other entities, yet the focus is still very much on ourselves. The goal is to turn everything around us, even God, into a means to our self-chosen ends. We love God for all that God can do for us.

The old reformer observed that stage two is about as far as the great host of humanity ever gets in its religious development. Individuals are aware of God, but they are intent on using the Holy One to fulfill their own agendas.

If we're at all honest, this stage has a ring of truth to it. Look for a moment at the shape of your prayers. Are they not filled with personal requests and even demands? "Give me this...protect me from that...grant me the desires of my heart."

I once knew a person who lost a child to a serious illness. She had tried her best to get God somehow to intervene and heal that beloved individual. When that didn't occur, this person responded in rage and bitterness. When she couldn't get God to jump through her hoops on her own schedule, she promptly broke off all diplomatic relations with the Holy One and became an angry cynic. This is what often comes of "the love of God for self's sake," for the simple reason that "God's ways are not our ways, nor are his thoughts our thoughts." He isn't finally a cosmic bellhop who responds dutifully to our commands. Although this stage represents progress over infantile narcissism, it remains a manipulative, utilitarian approach to God and will ultimately not really satisfy all the needs of our heart.

Bernard's third stage represents a quantum leap forward. He calls it "the love of God for God's sake." Here's when one senses that God has value, not just in terms of what God can do for us, but in terms of what God is in himself. There are reasons to worship God that have nothing to do with our needs, but only with the wonder of what God is. Here's the beginning of ecstasy and wonder, the kind of disinterestedness that develops when we finally get ourselves off our hands and exude joy. God didn't have to be the way God is; that such a wonder of Being does exist becomes the focus of one's delight.

One of my loveliest memories goes back to the time when my little girl was about four years old. I was hard at work in my study one morning when she quietly slipped in—still in her night clothes—and without a word, climbed up in my lap and laid her head on my shoulder.

"I'm really glad to see you," I said to her. "What can I do for you? What do you want?"

She paused for a moment and then said, "Nothing. I just wanted to be close to you, that's all."

The memory of that moment is still golden to me, for she wasn't there on any utilitarian mission—just the wonder of being with and sharing! That experience gave me such satisfaction that it pains me to realize how few times I've gone into God's presence in that spirit—without any purpose except to say, "I simply want to be with you and glory in what you are, not in what you do for me." This is "the love of God for God's sake," and if I'd been putting together this continuum instead of Bernard, I'd have made this the ultimate level. If we could ever get out of ourselves long enough to love God solely for what God is, I'd have seen that as the pinnacle of all our spiritual strivings.

Therefore, imagine my surprise when I found the old reformer putting a fourth stage above "the love of God for God's sake." Do you know what it was? "The love of self for God's sake." I was shocked at first, but as I began to reflect on it, I realized the wisdom of this profound man. Think about it for a moment. Who is the most difficult person in the world for you to love? Whom do you have the most trouble accepting, affirming, celebrating, and then embracing?

If your experience is anything like mine, you would have to admit it was yourself. One of my deepest issues with God goes back to the very first thing he did for me—namely, create me. For some reason, the body I have, the mind I was given, the family system into which I was born—none of these is easy for me to affirm. There's much about my very being that I simply don't like, and in this sense, I don't feel I am alone.

I imagine across the years I've asked a hundred people in counseling sessions the same question— "Are you talented?"—and I've yet to have one person respond with an unequivocal "Yes!" "Oh, no, I was behind the door when they passed out the gifts," they'd rather say. "I've no talents, really." Folk may see this as a form of humility, but the truth is, it's self-dislike, and it lies at the bottom of our relationship to God. We don't seem to believe that God really knew what he was doing when he created us.

I remember so well how this negative sense of self dominated my early childhood. I'd sit on the front porch back in the 1930s and daydream. I remember wishing that I was tall and thin, with straight black hair, and that my name was Dick. These were very real childhood desires, and do you realize what they imply? I didn't like the way I'd come up from "the gates of the morning"; that is, being a short and stocky boy named John with wavy brown hair. I didn't regard the way I came into history a good.

Thus, Bernard was right when he designated "the love of self for God's sake" as the highest stage of spiritual development. As I've said earlier, being able to regard our own creation the way Genesis says God regards it, as something "good, good, very, very, good," is the essence of Christian redemption. What this means in these parables is that each one of us, as we were created, is the treasure buried in the field, the pearl of great price, and the fish valuable enough to keep.

Thus, the way to fulfillment lies in affirming that what God did in creation was good, and in letting that become our joy as surely as the farmer, the pearl merchant, and the fishermen found their joy in what they discovered. Given that most of us have felt negative about ourselves, finding out how God feels about us may be the most surprising discovery we will ever make.

The last words of the parable about the end of the age are ominous indeed. They warn that the angels will come and separate the evil from the righteous, and throw the evil into a furnace of fire where they shall weep and gnash their teeth forever. Why did Jesus include this word of fearful judgment? To explain that our existence is a decisive affair. It is possible to come to the summum bonum and to be fulfilled. It's also possible to miss the point and come to an ultimate failure. But we must never forget that the purpose behind judgment is growth, not condemnation. God judges us in order to teach us something, not to blow the whistle on us forever.

I've long felt that God's judgment is more like a flower show than a police court. In the latter, the focus is on guilt and punishment, while in the former, the goal is learning more about moving toward perfection.

I have a cousin who excelled in flower arranging. She used to enter shows, not to be condemned or exonerated, but to let the judges teach her what they knew about the ideal. This is how I imagine God's involvement. Remember, it isn't his will that any should perish, but rather that all come to the joy of fulfillment. Therefore, God will do all God can to bring each one of us to this goal, but not even an omnipotent God can coerce us into such a reality against our wills. This is why I said that ours is a decisive existence.

C. S. Lewis is right, I believe, when he says that there will come a time in the Great-Not-Yet when either we will say to God, "Thy will be done," and enter into the joy of the Lord, or God will say with infinite sadness to us, "Thy will be done," and let us go back into the nothingness from whence we came. If we don't receive the gift of God's love, it can't be injected into us like penicillin. Thus, all these seemingly dark sayings about the End Time are not put there because God is a sadist about to explode in rage. They are a monument to human freedom, and are reminders that finally you and I have to decide about what God has already decided—namely, that He wants us to share His joy forever, provided we will accept His invitation. If we steadfastly refuse to say yes, no one in all the universe will be sadder than God. Nonetheless, the joy God sets before us can only be received, it can't be forced on a creature.

Some years ago I had a vivid dream. I had been reading Raymond Moody's small book *Life After Life,* which is a collection of several people's accounts of near-death experiences. This undoubtedly was at work in my subconscious and shaped the images I experienced. I dreamed I died physically, moved through a dark tunnel, and came out into what can best be described as "kindly light." There was no visible object or figure, only a great sense of warmth and acceptance. Then a Voice said, "Welcome, my child. I want to ask you some questions."

I stiffened in fright, and thought to myself, "Here comes the judgment and my condemnation."

But the Voice said, "First, I want to ask you, can you weep over all the mistakes you made, over all the pain you've caused other people, over all the ways you've failed to live up to your highest and best?"

I began to think about the many things in my life that were occasions for regret. Genuine tears begin to come up from the depths of my being, and I cried as if my heart would break.

But then the Voice spoke again. "Let me ask you something else. Can you laugh over all the good experiences you've had, at all the good jokes you heard, all the funny things that you've seen?"

Again, I began to remember back over all the joys of my life and started laughing as I'd never laughed before, and so help me, it seemed that that ocean of light was laughing with me! If you've never heard the laughter of God, you've missed something absolutely ecstatic.

Then the Voice spoke yet again. "I need to ask you one more question. This wonder of aliveness— do you want any more of it? Do you want to go on living?"

I remember thinking that this was no automatic issue. I really did have a choice! I pondered slowly all the pain and pleasure that I'd known from living, and then from the deepest place in my being I said, "Yes! Yes! I do want some more of it!"

With that the Voice exclaimed delightedly, "Come, then, you blessed of the Father, and enter into the joy of your Lord. Plunge deeper in and further on," and with that I swam off into the ocean of light.

I don't claim for this dream any ultimate authority, but I do believe it corresponds to the highest and deepest notes of the Christian vision. To enter the kingdom of Heaven, what could be more essential than being able to weep over our sins, to laugh appreciatively over all our good times, and to say from the depths of our beings, "Yes, Lord, I want more of it." That would be "loving self for God's sake," would it not? It represents the summum bonum about which these parables speak.

In God's eyes, we're all a treasure, a pearl of great price, a keeper!

In our own eyes, I wonder, how do we see ourselves?

# 2

## The Vineyard Owner and His Workers

### Matthew 20:1-16

*For the kingdom of heaven is like a landowner who went out early in the morning to hire laborers for his vineyard. After agreeing with the laborers for a denarius a day, he sent them into his vineyard. And going out about the third hour he saw others standing idle in the marketplace; and to them he said, "You go into the vineyard too, and whatever is right I will give you." So they went. Going out again about the sixth hour and the ninth hour, he did the same. And about the eleventh hour he went out and found others standing; and he said to them, "Why do you stand here idle all day?" They said to him, "Because no one has hired us." He said to them, "You go into the vineyard too." And when evening came, the owner of the vineyard said to his steward, "Call the laborers and pay them their wages, beginning with the last, up to the first." And when those hired about the eleventh hour came, each of them received a denarius. But when the first came, they supposed that they would receive more; and they likewise received each a denarius. And on receiving it they grumbled at the householder, saying, "These last worked only an hour, and you have made them equal to us who have borne the burden of the day and the scorching heat." But he replied to one of them, "Friend, I am doing you no wrong; did you not agree with me for a denarius? Take what belongs to you and go; I choose to give to this last as I give to you. Am I not allowed to do what I choose with what belongs to me? Or do you begrudge my generosity?" So the last shall be first, and the first last.*

—

The setting of this parable was quite familiar to first-century Palestinians. It was the harvest season for a grape crop. The owner of a vineyard got up before dawn and went to the center of the village where day laborers congregated, hoping to find employment for the twelve-hour workday. These were the folk who didn't have regular jobs, nor did they own any property. They were much like migrant workers of our day; that is, they were totally at the mercy of others for any sort of employment.

Let me pause to note that most of us have a deep aversion to this kind of powerlessness. In a profound sense, however, these individuals mirror the condition of each one of us in relation to life itself. In the basic structure of things, we're all beings who were called into existence by a power other than ourselves, and we live each moment by the grace and generosity of that One who wanted us to be. None of us willed our way into this existence, nor set in motion the process that called us out of nothing into being.

We're radically dependent on nature. The English word "dependent" comes from the Latin word meaning "to hang." We human beings depend like a chandelier, hanging, held in place by something other than itself. Should that something ever let it go, it has no power in and of itself to avoid crashing down into brokenness. Such an image, however, need not be depressive. The essence of Christian salvation lies in learning to trust that Greater Than Ourselves on whom we depend. Carlyle Marney used to say, "When I die, I am going to get to the place where I'll have to say, if there's anything else, it's up to God. I've no power to make anything else happen."

This, of course, is radical dependence, but to those who have learned to trust, this needn't be an experience of despair. If Jesus taught us anything at all, it's that when we get to the end of our ropes, we're not at the end of everything! There's Another at that point of utter extremity, and that Other One is good. In this light, dependence ceases to be a threat and becomes a comfort. But let us get on with the story.

When the vineyard owner arrived, he chose only a select few of those assembled to go to his field. For the sake of illustration, let us suppose that thirty of these workers were standing there. He picked out six and agreed to pay them the going wage of the day, a denarius, which was about enough to keep a peasant family going for a single day. Notice carefully that an injustice of sorts was done here, for thirty were available and only six were hired. You hear no word of protest, however, from the chosen ones at this juncture. They were more than pleased to have a whole day's work ahead of them and the promise of taking home something to their families in the evening.

This underlines the fact that our sense of justice is highly subjective. Most of us never complain about injustice when it falls in our favor. In the game of poker, the player who has four aces rarely calls for a redeal. Do you ever remember someone in such a situation saying, "Look, this isn't fair. I have this incredible hand. Let's reshuffle and start all over." That isn't the way human nature works, and I am intentionally emphasizing this point, for those who get most upset at the end of the day had no complaints when things were breaking in their favor.

As the story unfolded, the vineyard owner went back at nine o'clock in the morning and found a pool of laborers still standing in the square; he told six of these men to go to his vineyard, and he'd pay them an appropriate wage. At twelve noon and then at three o'clock in the afternoon he did the same thing. At five that evening, just one hour before the workday was to come to an end, the vineyard owner went back to the village square and encountered what had to be a minor miracle, if you stop to think about it. Amazingly, there were still six day laborers waiting there, hoping against hope that they could get some kind of work so that they could put something on the table for their families. People with less courage and tenacity would have given up in despair, but here were individuals who still waited in hope for eleven interminable hours!

The vineyard owner asked, "Why are you still here? Is it because you're lazy and don't want to work?"

"No, sir," they answered, "we're here because nobody's been willing to hire us."

"Go to my vineyard there, and I'll pay you what is appropriate and just."

Please note that, at this point in the parable, everybody is partially satisfied, for each one has received at least a portion of what it was that they had set out for before the rising of the sun. None were going to have to go home empty-handed to a houseful of hungry children.

Then, at the close of the day, the vineyard owner instructed his steward to call in all the laborers. "Pay those who've worked the least amount of time first and then pay the rest."

When these men who had worked just an hour came up to the paying station, they were given, to their astonishment, a whole denarius, the going wage for twelve hours' work. Needless to say, they were delighted. When the three o'clock crowd came in, they too got a whole denarius, as did the noon crowd, the nine A.M. crowd, and the six A.M. crowd. And at this point, all hell broke loose. Those who'd been hired first were livid and demanded an audience with the vineyard owner.

To his credit, the vineyard owner didn't hide behind his steward and let somebody else do his dirty work for him. "Listen, there's been no injustice here. I've paid you exactly what I agreed to pay you at six A.M."

And then he adds an interesting note. "Am I not free to do with my abundance what I want? Or do you begrudge me my generosity?" Deeper than the issues of justice or fairness or unfairness, this is a matter of generosity.

The first time I read this parable, I must admit it seemed to be rampantly unfair. I found myself saying, "But that isn't just!" But then it dawned on me that I was starting at the wrong place. If you and I'd earned our way into this world or had received our existence as some sort of entitlement, then there might be some validity to such a complaint. But the beginning point of this parable is grace, not entitlement, and the same is true of life as well. Birth is windfall, and life is gift! We were called out of nothing into being in an astonishing act of generosity for which we can claim no right. Once that becomes our central focus, it changes forever how we interpret things. If entitlement is your beginning point, you evaluate the particulars of your life from one vantage point. On the other hand, if grace is your starting point, everything is going to appear in a very different light.

There's another Jewish parable that both parallels and illumines Jesus's story. It has helped me to clarify my understanding greatly. This is about a Jewish farmer who lived in Poland. For generations before him, his family had been very poor. One night he was awakened by an angel of the Lord, who said: "You've found favor in the eyes of your Maker. He wants to do for you what he did for your ancestor Abraham. He wants to bless you. Therefore, make any three requests that you will of God, and he will be pleased to give them to you. There's only one condition; your neighbor will get a double portion of everything that is bequeathed to you."

Well, the farmer was so startled by all this that he woke up his wife and told her all about it. She insisted they put the whole thing to the test. So they prayed. "Oh, blessed God, if we could just have a herd of a thousand cattle, that would enable us to break out of the poverty in which we've lived for generations. That would be wonderful." No sooner had they said these words than they heard the sound of animal noises outside. Lo and behold, all around the house were a thousand magnificent animals!

During the next two days, the Jewish farmer hardly touched the ground. He divided his time between praising God for his great generosity and beginning to make practical provisions for this affluence.

On the third afternoon, he was up on a hill behind his house, trying to decide where to build a new barn, when for the first time, he looked across at his neighbor's field, and there stood out from the green hillside two thousand magnificent cattle. For the first time since the angel of the Lord had appeared, the joy within him evaporated, and a scowl of envy took its place. He went home that evening in a foul mood, refused to eat supper, and went to bed in an absolute rage. He couldn't fall asleep, because every time he closed his eyes, all he could see were the two thousand cattle of his neighbor.

Deep in the night, however, he remembered that the angel had said he could make three wishes. With that, he shifted his focus away from his neighbor and back to his own situation, and the old joy quickly returned. Digging into his own heart to find out what else he really wanted, he began to realize that in addition to some kind of material security, he had always wanted descendants to carry on his name into history. So he prayed a second time. "Gracious God, if it please thee, give me a child that I may have descendants." With that, he made love to his wife, and because of his experience with the cattle, he wasn't too surprised shortly thereafter to have her tell him that she was bearing in her body a life not her own.

The next months were passed in unbroken joy. The farmer was busy assimilating his newly acquired affluence, and looking forward to the great grace of becoming a parent. And on the night his first child was born, he was absolutely overjoyed. The next day was the Sabbath. He went to the synagogue, and at the time of the prayers of the people, he stood up and shared with the gathered community his great good fortune: now at last a child had been born into their home. He had hardly sat down, however, when his neighbor got up. "God has indeed been gracious to our little community. I had twin sons born last night. Thanks be to God." On hearing that, the farmer went home in an utterly different mood from the one in which he came. Instead of being joyful, he was filled with the canker of jealousy.

And this time, the dark emotions didn't abate. Late that evening, he made his third request of God, which was, "Please, gouge out my right eye."

No sooner had he said these words than the angel who started the whole process came again. "Why, son of Abraham, have you turned to such dark desirings?"

With pent-up rage, the farmer replied, "I can't stand to see my neighbor prosper. I'll gladly sacrifice half of my vision for the satisfaction of knowing that he'll never be able to look on what he has."

Those words were followed by a long silence, and as the farmer looked, he saw tears forming in the eyes of the angel.

"Why, O son of Abraham, have you turned the occasion to bless into a time of hurting? Your third request won't be granted, not because the Lord lacks integrity, but because he is full of mercy. However, know this, O foolish one, you've brought sadness, not only to yourself, but to the very heart of God."

Do you see the parallel between the two parables? In both cases, individuals had nothing, knew themselves to be powerless and undeserving, and then out of the blue, grace came cascading into their lives. As long as they stayed focused on what had been given them, their experience was one of incredible joy. In both cases, however, what had at first been the occasion of great celebration turned into something very different, because they gave way to the sidelong glance of envy! They began to compare what they had to what others had, rather than to what they had at the beginning, and in both cases it turned their joy into curdled bitterness.

If you want to be miserable, then compare what you have to what some others have. Invariably, there'll be someone who has done better than you, who may not have worked as hard, yet wound up with a better outcome. If you base your evaluating on the sidelong, comparative angle, I guarantee that you can find a way to make yourself miserable.

The whole issue of fairness comes back to the one question, "Compared to what?"

In any kind of evaluation, the selection of criteria is absolutely crucial. You may have heard about the man who went to work on Monday morning, and ritualistically asked his boss, "How is your wife?" He was startled when the boss shot back, "Compared to what?" One doesn't have to be a philosopher to realize that this second question is crucial. You see, compared to Marilyn Monroe, the boss would have answered the question one way. Compared to Mother Theresa, the response would have been altogether different. Any kind of interpretation hinges on the criterion you choose, and this is the crucial meaning that Jesus was trying to convey in this parable. If I compare what I had before December 15, 1930, when I was born, then all the particulars of my life look wonderful in relation to the nothing I was before birth. This body, this mind, this place in history—they are a windfall in relation to not getting to be at all. If, however, I begin comparing my body to Arnold Schwarzenegger's or my mind to Stephen Hawking's or my wealth to Ross Perot, what I am and what I have begin to look utterly different. Hence, a fail-safe recipe for joy is regarding one's life as a gift. A fail-safe recipe for misery is comparing one's self to someone else and forgetting what a grace life really is.

I've a minister friend who told about a wonderful family in his parish; they already had four children and awaited with delight the coming of a fifth child. Everyone gathered at the hospital the night she was born. She was perfect in every way except one—for some reason she had no arms and legs. The doctor couldn't account for this genetic abnormality. This was a family of great resilience and courage, so instead of spending a lot of energy feeling sorry for themselves, they took this little girl in her condition and set out to give her every advantage they possibly could under the circumstances. She lived to be twenty-one, and my minister friend said that she developed into one of the most scintillating and delightful human beings he had ever known. She had a brilliant mind, a wonderful sense of humor, and a great capacity for friendship, although never once in her twenty-one years was she able to dress herself or feed herself or do any of the things most of us tend to take for granted.

One Easter her older brother brought his room-mate home from college for the weekend. As a philosophy major, and a sophomore to boot, he was in the habit of putting life under a microscope and ana-lyzing everything critically. After witnessing this girl's life for three days, he asked her, "What keeps you from blowing up in anger at whatever kind of God would have let you be born into this world in this condition? How do you keep from exploding in rage?"

My minister friend said that this girl looked him dead in the eyes and said, "I realize that compared to what most people have, what I have doesn't seem like much. But listen, I wouldn't have missed being born for anything. I've been able to see. I've been able to hear. I've been able to smell, to taste, and to feel. I've been exposed to some of the world's great literature. I've heard some of the finest music ever composed. I've had some of the most wonderful friendships that anybody could ever have. I know what I have doesn't seem like much when compared to what other peo-ple have, but compared to never getting to be at all, I wouldn't have missed being born for anything!"

Where did this human being get the courage to

relish the life she was given?  Somewhere along the line, someone had taught her that life is gift and birth is windfall, and that when compared to not getting to be at all, simply being born is like winning the Irish Sweepstakes.  If you want a formula for making the best of the less-than-perfect and making the most of what you've been given, choose to compare your lot to what you were before you were born, and it will empower you every time.

In Jesus's parable, every one of the workers had occasion for gratitude if he had only remembered what it was like before dawn. And the vineyard owner is a beautiful image of human potential.  In the end he wasn't a perpetrator of injustice.  In truth, he was a model of how wealth can be used compassionately and creatively.  What he did for the last four groups of workers was motivated by sensitivity, not abstract justice.  He realized that all thirty of those men had families to feed and needed a whole denarius.  He was thinking about them, not the service he had received from them, in deciding to pay them as he did.  It was his generosity—not just the concept of fairness—that accounts for his action, and we would do well to learn from him and do likewise.

This virtue is illustrated beautifully in another Jewish parable about a father and two sons.  This man was an ideal mentor.  He took his boys to the fields as soon as they were big enough to walk and taught them all he knew about farming.  When he died, instead of dividing their inheritance, they continued to work together in partnership, each contributing his best gifts and both dividing each harvest down the middle. One of the brothers married and had eight children; the other remained a bachelor.

One night, during a particularly bountiful harvest, the bachelor brother thought to himself, "My brother has ten mouths to feed and I've only one. He really needs more of this harvest than I do. However, I know him. He is much too fair to renegotiate our agreement. I know what I'll do. I'll take some of my harvest and slip it over in his barn at night so he can have more for his family."

At the very same time, the married brother was thinking to himself, "God has blessed me with this fine family. My children will take care of us when I am old. My brother isn't as fortunate. He really needs more of this harvest to provide for his old age, but I know him. He's far too fair to renegotiate our agreement. I know what I'll do. I'll take some of my harvest and slip it into his barn to build up a nest egg for the future."

As you might expect, one night when the moon was full, these brothers came face-to-face, each on a mission of mercy. And the old rabbi said that although there wasn't a cloud in the sky, a gentle rain began to fall. Do you know what it was? It was God weeping for joy! The real secret of human joy is sharing what we have with others rather than hoarding everything for ourselves.

I imagine the same God wept for joy over the

actions of that vineyard owner that late afternoon. He, too, modeled what it means to be made in the image of a generous God. And the truth is that we're all chips off that same beloved Block!

# 3

# The Talents

## Matthew 25:14-30

*For it will be as when a man going on a journey called his servants and entrusted to them his property; to one he gave five talents, to another two, to another one, to each according to his ability. Then he went away. He who had received the five talents went at once and traded with them; and he made five talents more. So also, he who had the two talents made two talents more. But he who had received the one talent went and dug in the ground and hid his master's money. Now after a long time the master of those servants came and settled accounts with them. And he who had received the five talents came forward, bringing five talents more, saying, "Master, you delivered to me five talents; here I have made five talents more." His master said to him, "Well done, good and faithful servant; you have been faithful over a little, I will set you over much; enter into the joy of your master." And he also who had the two talents came forward saying, "Master, you delivered to me two talents; here I have made two talents more." His master said to him, "Well done, dood and faithful servant; you have been faithful over a little, I will set you over much;*

*enter into the joy of your master." He also who had received the one talent came forward, saying, "Master, I knew you to be a hard man, reaping where you did not sow, and gathering where you did not winnow; so I was afraid, and I went and hid your talent in the ground. Here you have what is yours." But his master answered him, "You wicked and slothful servant! You knew that I reap where I have not sowed, and gather where I have not winnowed? Then you ought to have invested my money with the bankers, and at my coming I should have received what was my own with interest. So take the talent from him, and give it to him who has the ten talents. For to everyone who has, more will be given, and he will have abundance; but from him who has not, even what he has will be taken away. And cast the worthless servant into the outer darkness; there men will weep and gnash their teeth."*

—

A talent was originally a unit of measurement, like a gram or an ounce of precious metal. In Jesus's story this is the way it's used, but the parable has become so well known to English-speaking people that "talent" has come to mean any capacity or ability that a human being believes that he or she has received from God. We no longer think of a talent as just a unit of gold or silver. We talk about musical talent, artistic talent, athletic talent. I point this out simply to remind us of the enormous influence this story has had on the shaping of our Western understanding to our own day. Its images speak directly to our era of human history. Therefore, let us look at the story carefully to see where we can find ourselves reflected in it and discover some resources for our own growth. Here's how Jesus began.

The people to whom Jesus first spoke these words were very familiar with this practice. Wealthy people turned over their property to trusted servants before departing on long journeys. Because travel was so uncertain back then, there was no way of knowing how long they'd be gone, or if they'd ever come back.

These wealthy people fell into two groups, merchants and rulers. The merchants had to journey to other places to secure their goods, some going as far as India and parts of southern Europe. The provincial rulers in the system of the Roman Empire, mostly tax collectors, were summoned to Rome from time to time.

One such example would have been the son of Herod the Great, a man named Archelaus. In 4 B.C., a shift of imperial power occurred, and he had to return to Rome to secure his right to continue the oversight of Judea and Samaria. He undoubtedly went through the very routine that Jesus described here. He called his most trusted lieutenants and made each one of them responsible for certain parts of his holdings. He'd have charged them to do what they had seen him doing and be ready to give an accounting when he returned.

Incidentally, there's a funny side to Archelaus's particular situation. He had created quite a few enemies, as all rulers are likely to do. Thus, when he went to Rome to secure his claim on the future, fifty Jews also went to the Emperor to protest his fitness as a ruler and to ask that another be appointed in his place. When the Emperor ruled in favor of Archelaus, those fifty folk wisely decided not to return home! In other words, they had left their property under someone else's control and never went back to see about it.

Such an image isn't only reflective of the way things were done in that era; it also reflects accurately the way the Hebrews understood the relation of God to history and to human beings. Creation was originally an act of divine generosity, where the Holy One set out to enable creatures in his own image to experience the kind of joy that was uniquely God's. This meant that such beings would necessarily have to possess certain characteristics, if the divine goal were to be achieved. They'd need power—the ability to do things, to make things happen. They'd need freedom, for no robot could experience God's kind of personal ecstasy. And they'd need the quality of spirit that God possesses, which finds delight in doing the things that both please the actors and bless all who are affected by such actions. God's particular kind of joy is made up of these three components, all of which necessitate a certain way of God relating to the human creatures.

Gettis MacGregor has written a wonderful little book entitled *He Who Lets Us Be*. His premise is that

God shows his love for us as much in what he does not do for us as in what he does do. He says if your only understanding of divine compassion is that of God always hovering over you like a mother over an infant, then you're only seeing one aspect of His reality. MacGregor quotes with great appreciation Simone Weil's well-known dictum, "Creation was the moment when God ceased to be everything so we humans could become something."

In other words, for humans to develop fully, God must back away from us and allow us to move on our own. How would a baby ever learn to walk if its parents continued to carry it everywhere? By putting the child down and moving away, the possibility of personal growth begins. Thus, God's distancing Himself from us isn't a sign of desertion or abandonment, but precisely an expression of a love that wills us to grow. This is how the Hebrews understood the dynamics of creation. It corresponds beautifully with Jesus's analogy of a rich man handing over certain powers and freedoms and then going away. When God ceased to be the sole actor on the stage of history, our chance to become actors too was born. It's God's plan, then, that we grow up under his loving eye but not under his domineering thumb. This is the framework Jesus set forth in this story of God's relation to us humans and our relation to God.

But then the story unfolds. One servant was entrusted with five talents, another with two, and another with only one talent, each according to his ability. Here's yet another accurate reflection of our human condition. Søren Kierkegaard, a Danish philosopher who was much given to paradox, once observed that we humans are at once "exactly alike and utterly different." He insisted that one must hold both of those ideas together simultaneously or the uniqueness of our human situation will become distorted. I think this is correct, although it's never easy to embrace at one time what seems on the surface to be contradictory.

Years ago, when I was in graduate school and reading a lot of Kierkegaard, I was flying on a plane with an old professor, and we were discussing this very issue. "Isn't paradox," I asked, "the basic form of all finite knowledge?"

He looked out the window for a long time, and then he replied. "Yes and no!"

His answer, of course, confirmed my point. Yet how can we humans be exactly alike and at the same time utterly different? Let's look at these three individuals whom Jesus identifies in this parable. There's a sense in which each one of them is exactly alike, in that each received his opportunity because of the action of another. None of these individuals possessed anything of their own. What they had was bequeathed to them by this owner.

By this same token, each one of them was given the same mandate; namely, that they were to imitate what they had seen the master doing while he was there in their presence. They were to perpetuate the process that he had set in motion.

Each one was also told that when the owner came back, they'd be accountable for what was entrusted to them. It's in these senses that all three were exactly alike, and truth be told, the same can be said about all of us.

Every one of us was given our chance to live by the action of Another. We didn't engineer our birth into the world—it was a gift, a sheer, total, unmerited gift. We were all given the same mandate as well—to do with our gifts and powers what God does with His. And the note of accountability also applies to each of us all. God isn't an irresponsible or indifferent Giver. He is going to want to know at the end of our journey what we've done with all He gave us in the beginning. In these senses we humans are all alike.

At the same time, these three were markedly different from each other in that one had responsibility for five talents, another two, and another only one. And again, this is an accurate reflection of our situation, for while we're alike in our relation to and dependency on God, we're very different in terms of our natural capabilities, backgrounds, and the opportunities we have. Humankind has not been created equal in this regard.

There was a wonderful old black man who worked for my grandfather all his life on a farm in Kentucky. I'm not sure he had more than a third-grade education. He used to pride himself on having been born on the same day and year as Franklin Delano Roosevelt. I used to hear this old gentleman brag about his similarity to our revered President, but what a difference of opportunities opened out before those two individuals who entered history at the same moment!

But let's move on and reflect on the way these three servants responded to this challenge. The one who had received five talents went out at once and put these resources to work. This is what his mentor had always done, and before long he had turned the five talents into ten. The one that received the two talents did exactly the same thing, but the servant who received only one talent responded in a very different fashion. He dug a hole in the ground and buried his master's money.

After a considerable period, the landowner returned to settle up all accounts. When the five-talent man went forward bringing five talents more, the landowner exclaimed, "Well done, good and faithful servant!" I hear in this an echo from Genesis 1, where God looked on what he had done and exclaimed, "It's good! It's good! It's very, very good!" The master went on. "You've been faithful over a little, I'll set you over even more. Come, you blessed one, enter into the joy of your master."

The man who had been given two talents went forward showing the same results, and he was given an identical affirmation and invitation to move deeper into the joy of his master.

When the last servant reported in, however, his was a very different story. "Master, I knew you to be a hard man, reaping where you didn't sow and gathering where you didn't winnow, so I was afraid. I went out and hid your talent in the ground. Here you have back what is yours."

At this, the master exploded. "You wicked and slothful servant! If you thought I reaped where I'd not sown and gathered where I'd not winnowed, at least you ought to have invested my money with the bankers, so that at my returning I'd have received what was my own with interest. Take the talent from this one," he commanded, "and give it to him who has ten talents, for lo, everyone who has will be given more and he shall have in abundance, but from him who hasn't, even what he has will be taken away. Remove this worthless servant from me. He is totally out of sync with the dynamics of this process."

What are we to make of these images? I think they confirm the fact that we're made in the image of a dynamic and creative God, and that we do taste God's kind of ecstasy when we imitate with our powers what we see God doing with His. The two servants who were energetic and creative with their gifts modeled what God had in mind for the creation from the very first. This universe about us is full of mystery indeed, but I think you can count on the fact that it's finally a fair and faithful place, when you follow the example of the Holy One described so beautifully in Genesis. God freely used His power to delight

Himself and bless all He touched, and this is the pattern we're all to follow as well.

This does not mean you'll always at every moment get exactly what you think you want. There are many mysterious zigzags in the course of history, but at bottom there's also a faithfulness between what we sow and what we reap.

I remember some years ago reading a memorial oration that C. S. Lewis gave at King's College, the University of London. He called it "The Inner Ring." He told these highly privileged, well-placed young students that because of their education they'd have great access to the corridors of power in that culture. He suggested two ways they could approach their destiny.

One way would be that of manipulation—to work first this angle and then that angle to finagle one's way into as much power as possible as quickly as possible. Those who take this shortcut to influence, however, would not likely develop the kind of skills that heavy responsibility ultimately demands.

The other route, Lewis contended, was to resolve to do good work, to take whatever was one's chosen discipline and learn how to do it thoroughly and well. This approach would be much slower, but in the end, other good workmen would recognize the quality of their labors and grant them access to real power.

This is ultimately the only way into the true inner ring, and I don't see that as a false or elusive promise.

When one resolves to become a good craftsperson in whatever gift, there'll come a time when others will recognize this fact, and the influence of such effort will have a more lasting effect. The point is, this is a faithful and fruitful universe.

In Jesus's parable, the owner wasn't as interested in the quantity of what each had as in their faithfulness to do good work with their opportunities. It follows that God isn't going to ask for the same results from each one of us, because we've not all been given the same abilities or opportunities. What will be asked is, "What have you done with what you were given?"

There's a wonderful old rabbinical parable to the effect that when one comes before the judgment seat of God, he won't ask, "Why weren't you Abraham?" or "Why weren't you Moses?" What he will want to know is, "Were you yourself? Did you do the best you could with what you had?" Remember, the whole purpose of existence is for us to experience God's kind of joy, and the secret here is to use our power and freedom the way God uses His—to delight Himself and bless all others.

Let's look now at the shadowed side of this parable—the third servant who was given only one talent and didn't do a thing with it. Here's a somber warning, I believe. There are two ways of being unfaithful, actually. There's the hot way, which is to abuse our powers and use them destructively. This is the sin of commission. And then there's the cold way of being unfaithful, which is to do nothing at all and therefore neglect and abort one's potential.

Interestingly enough, in one of the Apocryphal Gospels, there's a parable almost identical to this one, except that the servant takes the one talent and goes out and wastes it on wine and women. When the master returns, the servant hasn't a thing to show. This shows the abusive use of power. The unfaithfulness we see in this parable, however, is that of a man who had done none of these things. His mistake was that he did nothing at all, simply burying what he had been given and neglecting it. This is the sin of omission, and it's just as serious, although its true effect is much slower in coming to light. The people who do nothing are never caught off base or red-handed, so it's very easy for them to be critical of the folks who are trying to do things but who visibly fail.

If you'll look carefully at the teachings of Jesus, he took the sin of underutilizing what you could be just as seriously as the sin of overutilizing in abuse. Sin is finally a matter of trying to be either more or less than we ought to be, and either way it's a "falling short of the glory," as St. Paul put it in Romans 3:23.

Because of the seriousness of this issue, let us look more closely at what may have caused this tragic missing of the mark. What went wrong so to abort the divine pattern of things? The most obvious explanation here is simple inertia; that is, the servant didn't want to put forth the effort to undertake a more creative route. Burying his talent in the ground was the lazy way of handling his responsibility.

Scott Peck goes so far as to say that inertia may be the essence of original sin. He points to the second chapter of Genesis, where the serpent made certain damaging accusations against God. Peck makes the following point. If the first man and woman had proceeded to research the matter energetically—that is, if they had gone to God and said, "Let us tell you what the serpent said about you and is it true?"— they could have easily discovered that they were being told a pack of lies. However, that is precisely what they did not do! They lazily accepted without investigation what the serpent had implied and proceeded to act on it.

Will Durant makes the same point in his *Lessons of History*; he affirms that what finally makes the difference in all the cultures of history comes down to the issue of energy. Those who put forth the most effort achieved the greatest results, and this may finally explain the failure of that servant. He chose not to bestir himself as the others did, but to follow the way of a layabout and do nothing.

A second possibility, however, may have been jealousy and envy. He was bound to have noticed what was entrusted to his other colleagues, and might have focused more energy on the hands they had been dealt than on the possibilities that were his to exercise. The sidelong glance is a sure way to lose one's focus and get deflected from one's own mission. Jesus reminded Simon Peter of that right before His

Ascension. The two had reconciled by the Sea of Galilee. Jesus totally forgave Peter and set him once again to the task of feeding his sheep. It was a high moment of reconciliation.

But then seeing John, Peter began to inquire as to his destiny. Jesus retorted bluntly, "That's none of your business, Peter. You've your task to perform. Focus on that, and not idle speculation!" (John 21:22) It could be that this is what deflected the focus of the third servant. What the others got caused him to lose sight of his responsibility.

A third possibility may have been that the smallness of his talent led him to conclude that what he did with it didn't matter. If I believe anything at all, it's that in God's universe, there's nothing that is totally insignificant. The great things were first of all little things that were lifted up to God in reverence and gratitude and then used to the fullest. It's a mistake to confuse size with value.

Bob Benson recognized this fact quite clearly. He tells about his son turning up with a bit part in an elementary school play. The lad had hoped for better things, but he was relegated to having only two lines close to the end of the whole production. The performance took place on a hot May evening, and this is what Benson wrote in his journal that night. "Mike wasn't a star, by any means, but he waited faithfully, and when his moment came, he was ready. He said his lines, and he said them well—not too soon, not too late, not too loud, not too soft, but just right."

Then Benson went on to reflect. "I am just a bit player too, not a star in any sense of the word, but God gave me a line or so in the pageant of life, and when the curtain falls and the drama ends and the stage is vacant at last, I don't ask for the critic's rave or fame in any amount. My only hope is this—that I can hear from afar the voice of God saying, 'He said his lines and he said them well—not too soon, not too late, not too loud, not too soft. He said his lines, and he said them well!'"

There's nothing too small from the hand of God. I can't help but wonder, however, if this one-talent man failed to realize the incredible significance of the tiny things that were given to him.

Any of these factors could account for his missing the mark, I suppose, but the text itself suggests that the real problem was one of mistrust. The servant acknowledged as much when he said to the owner, "I took you to be a hard man." He went on to accuse him of being dishonest, and then claimed he was afraid; that was why he buried the talent. "Who knows what you would have done to me if I'd lost it?" he asked. "Here, take it back, just as you gave it."

Once again, we encounter that greatest of all dehumanizers—fear. Nothing distorts our humanity quite as much as the sense that there isn't enough and therefore one has to fight or flee. And, of course, more than anything else, this is what Jesus came to cast out. The serpent got the whole human race off track by casting false aspersions on God's character. He projected onto God what this servant projected onto his master—God was hard, cruel, dishonest, and untrustworthy. It was to undo this misrepresentation that Jesus was brought into history.

John Killinger claims, "Jesus was God's answer to the problem of a bad reputation," and reconciliation finally occurs when we let Jesus show us the Father and disprove forever the serpent's distortion. What this servant did out of fear is an analogy of what we humans do when we picture God fearfully instead of lovingly. We not only violate our own natures, by becoming either more or less than we are; we also unmake the whole creation that God has so carefully crafted. This is why Jesus takes the actions of this fearful servant so seriously. That fate of being cast into utter darkness isn't meant to describe what God wants at all, but rather how important it is that we see God's true nature and then begin to live our lives accordingly. "It isn't the will of the Father that any shall perish," Jesus said (Matthew 18:14). To warn against this and to show the way of salvation is why He told this parable.

It isn't too late for anyone. We all can see what Jesus came into the world to show—the Fatherly nature of God—and then begin to act out of love and not fear.

Well, what are we waiting for?

# 4

# The Final Judgment

## Matthew 25:31-46

*When the Son of man comes in His glory, and all the angels with Him, then He will sit on His glorious throne. Before Him will be gathered all the nations, and He will separate them one from another as a shepherd separates the sheep from the goats, and He will place the sheep at His right hand, but the goats at the left. Then the King will say to those at His right hand, "Come, O blessed of My Father, inherit the kingdom prepared for you from the foundation of the world; for I was hungry and you gave Me food, I was thirsty and you gave Me drink, I was a stranger and you welcomed Me, I was naked and you clothed Me, I was sick and you visited Me, I was in prison and you came to Me." Then the righteous will answer Him, "Lord, when did we see Thee hungry and feed Thee, or thirsty and give Thee drink? And when did we see Thee a stranger and welcome Thee, or naked and clothe Thee? And when did we see Thee sick or in prison and visit Thee?" And the King will answer them, "Truly, I say to you, as you did it to one of the least of these my brethren, you did it to Me." Then He will say to those at His left hand,*

*"Depart from Me, you cursed, into the eternal fire pre-*
*pared for the devil and his angels; for I was hungry and*
*you gave Me no food, I was thirsty and you gave Me no*
*drink, I was a stranger and you did not welcome Me,*
*maked and you did not clothe Me, sick and in prison*
*and you did not visit Me." Then they will also answer,*
*"Lord, when did we see Thee hungry or thirsty or a*
*stranger or naked or sick or in prison, and did not min-*
*ister to Thee?" Then He will answer them, "Truly, I say*
*to you, as you did it not to one of the least of these, you*
*did it not to Me." And they will go away into eternal*
*punishment, but the righteous into eternal life.*

———

If I had to pick the three most influential parables
that Jesus ever told, I'd have to include this story of
the final judgment as remembered in Matthew's
Gospel. In my opinion, no set of images Jesus ever
used has shaped Western civilization more profoundly
than this one. The sentiment, "In as much as you've
done it to the least of these my brethren, you've done
it unto Me," has found its way into many places and
has been highly significant in the formation of
Christian behavior. Here's one of Jesus's most powerful truths, and for that reason we need to look at it
most carefully.

It would be very easy to read this parable and miss
the gospel. In point of fact, many people have done
just that and reduced Christian faith to nothing
more than a call for humanitarian activity. They've
turned Christian salvation into something one earns

by virtue of how much good one does. For this reason, it's important that we not fall prey to such a misreading of this important part of Jesus's teaching.

Here, as always, our Lord took some familiar first-century Palestinian images and used them, first to intrigue his hearers, then at the proper moment to surprise them by revealing to them something they very much needed to learn. Please keep in mind that Jesus lived in an agricultural society, where growing food and taking care of animals were the main ways of earning a living.

In that era, sheep and goats ate the same kind of grass, so it was quite common for one shepherd to have both as part of his flock. At sundown, however, all of that changed, for the two species of animals had very different nighttime needs. Goats didn't have very thick hair, which meant they needed more protection against the chill of the night air. On the other hand, sheep were covered with a heavy coat of wool and could easily spend the night in the open. Goats needed to be taken to shelter each evening while sheep did not.

Yet another differential was that sheep were much more valuable than goats. They were capable of producing a coat of wool each year which could be sheared and sold, and then, after many seasons of that kind of production, slaughtered and sold for food. A goat, on the other hand, had much less economic value, their milk being their only source of producing a profit. It follows from such a distinction that much more attention was paid to sheep than to goats, and the task of separating them from each other at the end of the day was a common procedure.

This was made easier because, by and large, Palestinian goats were usually black and Palestinian sheep usually white. There were some exceptions to this, of course, but it wasn't that hard, even in the deepening shadows, to distinguish the one from the other.

Jesus took this familiar pastoral practice and proceeded to use it as an analogy for what was going to happen when the sun goes down on history; that is, when the day of our living in time and space draws to a close. His metaphor for this event is, "When the Son of Man comes in His glory."

C. S. Lewis says if you know much about the theater, you realize that when the author steps on the stage, the play is over! Here the Author of history comes on stage and proceeds to bring all that has been said and done to a point of climatic evaluation. To put it in a contemporary image, at the sunset of history, there's going to be a final examination of all of us—an accounting as to what we've done with our days and our nights. Such an awesome climax to history is what this parable is all about.

Let me step back for just a moment and, before we get to the particulars of this story, ask you honestly, How does such a prospect make you feel, this image of some being sent to the right and some to the left? Here, again, is Jesus's assertion that human existence is a decisive affair, that we do have choices and that real consequences grow out of how we exercise our freedom. I think Jesus is warning us here that ultimate failure is a possibility, that nothing is automatic in this kind of world.

I don't see how one can read this parable and not sense that Jesus is at least alerting us to the fact that tragedy is one of the options that lies out ahead of every human being. This existence of ours has a decisive character to it. What we do does make a difference. Our lives really are going somewhere. This world isn't a fool's paradise, where anything you do is going to come out the same. What we do or fail to do is a crucial component in the shaping of our destiny. It isn't the only factor, thanks be to God, but it is a crucial one.

Across the centuries, real effort has been expended to soften the implications of these last two assertions. Some say that even though human existence is decisive, God's grace is so powerful and so ingenious that failure and tragedy are not ultimate possibilities, that somehow grace will win out and everything will end on a totally positive note. The theological word for this position is called "universalism," and what it means is that in the end every person will finally be saved, every creature finally brought back home, and there will be no permanent failure or ultimate tragedy.

There's no question that certain verses in Holy Scripture seem to support such an optimistic view.

For example, Jesus didn't die in a condemning mode at all, but expressing what appears to be everlasting mercy: "Father forgive them, for they know not what they do." In John's Gospel, Jesus is remembered as having said, "And I, if I be lifted up from the earth, will draw all men to Myself" (12:32). That is, eventually what He has done in His costly act of love will have a redemptive impact on every person.

St. Paul picks up this note, and in some of his writings, appears to embrace universalism. "For as in Adam, all die," he says, "so also in Christ shall all be made alive" (I Corinthians 15:22). In his letter to the Philippians, he quotes a hymn that was in wide use in the first century, to the effect that "every knee will bow and every tongue confess that Jesus is Lord" (Philippians 2:10-11). Again in his Corinthian correspondence, Paul says that in the end the last enemy of God will be overcome. All evil will be swallowed up, then everything will be given back to the Father, and God will become all-in-all, everything to everyone (I Corinthians 15:26-28). So, let it be admitted that there are several portions of Scripture that do affirm that grace is going to triumph and that finally the ingenious mercy of God is going to win back every creature whom God has ever created.

Let me go on to say that I hope with all my heart that this is true. I wrote my doctoral dissertation back in 1959 on "The Problem of Hell in Contemporary Theology." I took the theological writings from Karl Barth's *Commentary on Romans* down to the present day and studied carefully this whole issue of the shape of the ultimate outcome of history. One of the things I discovered was that many people were emotionally offended by the thought of such a positive possibility. In other words, they seem to feel that if everybody gets in, then it's hardly worth being there. I detected a kind of fraternity/sorority mentality, which says that the joy of being in lies in the fact that most people are out.

I want to confess having a very different set of feelings. If the final outcome of history is totally positive, I'll be totally delighted! There isn't a thing in me that wants to see any part of creation left out. Having said that, however, if you take seriously the whole sweep of the biblical vision, I simply don't see how you can say dogmatically, "This is the way it has got to come out." I say this for two very powerful reasons.

First of all, if human freedom is genuine and God really did give us genuine autonomy when God called us into being, and if love is noncoercive, how can you unequivocally assert that everybody is going to do a certain thing? Grace isn't a bulldozer that finally makes people do something, whether they're willing or not. This has to be taken seriously in thinking out this issue. I hope with all my heart that love finds a way to woo freely every single soul back to God, but to assert dogmatically that this has to happen seems to go against the grain, not only of this parable, but of the whole tenor of Holy Scripture. "Choose you this day whom you will serve" (Joshua 24:15) is a meaningless imperative if human beings have no freedom, or if God is finally going to force us to end up at a certain place. Universalism may be a more loving form of determinism than predestination, but it's still a determinism. Such a view does violence to both the mystery of the divine and the human as they're depicted in the biblical vision.

The feel for life in this parable is true to existence as you and I experience it and true to the overall sweep of the biblical vision. Human existence is decisive. It does matter what we do. Failure is a possibility, and ultimate tragedy is one of the options that is open for every one of us.

If a human being, however, does fail to come to the goal God wants, who is to blame for this? Once again, the biblical witness is complex and multifaceted. Certain portions of Holy Scripture seem to imply that God has a limited amount of mercy and patience. If humans continue to thwart him, the Holy One finally "gives up" and proceeds understandably to blow up in frustration over our unwillingness to let him have his way.

The problem, then, is both human intractability and the limited supply of God's mercy. I, however, don't see the issue this way. The adjective that is most often coupled with the noun "mercy" in the Old Testament is the word "everlasting," and the adjective most often linked with God's love is "steadfast." In the Prayer of Humble Access in the Episcopal *Book of Common Prayer,* we acknowledge that we are "unworthy even to pick up the crumbs under God's table," but then we appeal to the One "whose property is always to have mercy." The word "always" is crucial, suggesting that God never runs out of patience and mercy.

Matthew 18:14 is my North Star when it comes to getting my bearings theologically. "It is not the will of the Father that even one of these little ones should perish." What God creates, God loves, and what God loves, God loves everlastingly. Therefore, if there's an ultimate failure, I don't think we can rightly lay the charge at God's feet, except for the fact that God is the One that gave us freedom in the first place and set this whole adventure into motion. No, if there's ultimate failure, it can better be traced back to our own freedom and to our own unwillingness to say "yes" to the gift of existence that God wants to give us. You see, if there's nothing about the way it is that pleases me, if my chance to be alive, if the body, the mind, the opportunities that were given me, if all are regarded negatively, there's nothing even an omnipotent God can forcibly do to alter this.

You may be familiar with the name of Jean-Paul Sartre, the French existentialist who wrote extensively in the '40s and '50s. Toward the end of his life, he wrote an autobiography and gave it the one word title *Nausea!* After pondering all his days and nights, his ultimate reaction was, "The whole thing makes me want to throw up!" This was his final estimate of life in all it facets. Isn't it clear, then, that sheer brute force is powerless to create joy in certain people?

I've referred before to C.S. Lewis's conclusion that either we say to God "Thy will be done" and enter into the joy of the Lord, or God says to us with infinite sadness the same words and lets us go back into the nothingness from whence we came. This would be an eternal punishment, but not be an eternal punishing. I personally can't conceive of a just God calling a creature into existence and this creature saying, "I don't want to live; I don't like anything about life"— and of such a God continuing to hold this soul in an existence of unending torture and pain. No decent human being would treat a dog like that! Therefore, I don't believe God is going to subject people forever to some kind of senseless torture simply out of frustration.

I do think, however, that if we had said in a million ways "I don't want to be—I don't want to have anything to do with the gift of existence as You're giving it," even God would realize that He doesn't have the power to make us experience joy if we refuse to do so. This is why letting us go back into the nothingness from whence we came is the only compassionate solution. God will always remember sadly; "I wanted that person to know My infinite joy, but even I cannot force this attitude on another."

Similarly, as He berated Jerusalem and said from the depths of His heart, "Jerusalem, Jerusalem, how

I'd have gathered you like a hen gathers her chicks, but you wouldn't let me!" There will always be grief in the heart of God over our unwillingness to let the gift of life be the joy He wanted it to be.

But how does this square with the images in the parable in which the evil spend eternity "weeping and wailing and gnashing of teeth"? I think these refer not to some punishment that is inflicted upon us after death, but to the quality of experience that results from disliking every aspect of God's gift to us. If nausea is your primary metaphor for life, then that is compatible with the images of anguish in the parable. Notice carefully, however, that this does not grow out of God's being vindictive, but our decision to dislike life the way it is. This isn't what God desires for anyone, mind you. If it occurs, it will be literally over God's dead body; that is, the action of Jesus on the cross. In that event, love did everything love is capable of doing and still remain love. To coerce would be to violate the very nature of love, and this God will not do.

Let me underline that God does not want this dark destiny for anyone, and this parable is one of the strategies that Jesus employs to effect that end. Therefore, one way of understanding this parable is to maintain Jesus giving us the final exam in the middle of the course. He is telling us in advance, "This is what is going to be most important in the end." He is doing this so that we can get the point and use our freedom to opt for joy.

As I've said before, God's purpose in acts of judgment is to teach us something rather than condemn us. One of the finest professors I ever had taught Greek and Latin at Baylor University. A learned man, a former Rhodes Scholar, he had a passion to communicate what he knew to others. He'd prepare us quite thoroughly for all our tests; as soon as we finished, he had us bring him our papers and would proceed to grade them while we stood there. I can still see his red pencil marking each mistake, but it didn't stop there. He took that occasion to teach us the right answer. You see, his purpose wasn't giving out grades or flunking people; he was there to share the wonder and wisdom of an ancient language. Even the act of testing was a mechanism for teaching.

It's in this sense that we can best understand the parable of the last judgment. Jesus is giving us the final exam well in advance, precisely because He wants us to pass it with flying colors! Its purpose isn't to condemn us, but to give us a sense of where we are in our own development and the direction in which we need to grow. I'm not trying to be cute when I say that the purpose of this parable isn't to scare the Hell out of us, but rather to inspire us to grow in the direction of heavenly joy!

What, then, is the continuum of perfection or wholeness that underlines this human existence of ours? What would it mean to move step by step from the beginning to the kind of fulfillment that God desires for each one of us? The biblical vision, it seems to me, is centered in the reality of love, and we need to consider very carefully the precise nature of this reality.

One of the last books C. S. Lewis ever wrote was called *The Four Loves*; in it he makes a primal distinction between what he calls "need-love" and "gift-love." I'd like to place these realities side by side so as to construct a continuum of spiritual development.

Need-love is something that is born of emptiness, something that is always on the lookout for values that can fill it. This involves seeing something in another person or object that is highly appealing and immediately reaches out to possess the beloved and import some of that value back into itself. Need-love is by nature a circular affair—it goes out of itself for the purpose of returning to itself with whatever it has gained. Need-love, therefore, is always acquisitive. Its goal is to get something for itself. The transfer of value here is always from the object to the subject.

Lewis observes that much of what goes on in the name of love is actually this sort of transaction. When a person says, "I love you," they may well be saying, "I need you, I want you, I desire to take something of what you are and try to fill the emptiness inside myself." Think of the times we've all loved something because the beloved had a value we wanted to acquire. Who can claim to be complete stranger to this form of loving?

Alongside need-love, however, Lewis describes a very different sort of thing called gift-love. It does belong on the opposite end of the continuum, for instead of being born of emptiness, it's born of fullness. Instead of reaching out to get, this kind of love reaches out to give. Instead of being a circle that goes out to come back, gift-love is an arc—it flows out simply to confer value, not to extract it. If the transfer of value in need-love is from object to subject, with gift-love the transfer is from subject to object. Its sole agenda is to enhance the value of the beloved, not to acquire value from the beloved. If a vacuum is a natural symbol for need-love, an overflowing artesian well is the symbol for gift-love. It is essentially creative rather than extractive, the epitome of generosity rather than exploitation.

Once you get this distinction clearly in mind, Lewis says that the best way to sum up the essence of the Christian vision is to say God's love is gift-love, not need-love. God's reason for creating was to give something of God's self, not to get something for himself. There was no emptiness in the Holy One that He attempted to fill by making the world. There was an ampleness in this One that made Him want to overflow in the confidence there was more where that came from. The deepest truth of the Gospel is that this is who God is and that we're made in the image of such a One. When you apply this vision to the images of this parable, it begins to come to life in a beautiful and inspiring way.

For example, Jesus says to all of those on the right: "Come, you blessed of My Father, and inherit the kingdom prepared for you from the foundations of the world. I was hungry and you gave Me to eat, thirsty and you gave Me to drink, naked and you clothed Me, a stranger and you welcomed Me, in prison and you came to Me." Here were certain people who didn't possess any notable value—the hungry, the thirsty, the naked, and the sick. They have little to give if getting something was the motive of those on the right.

On the contrary, these folk had discovered that they were made in the image of gift-love, so like artesian wells, they overflowed freely and joyfully and transferred some of their value over to those who really needed it. Their goal was to enhance these struggling people, not to exploit them. Because they were utterly unself-conscious in what they were doing, it is clear that they really were operating out of a gift-love stance. Had they been seeking to gain something in all this, they'd have been anxious to get recognition. But when Jesus explained to them why they were inheriting the kingdom, they were amazed; they revealed they had not been trying to gain anything at all. Then Jesus said, "That's precisely the point. You were doing what you were doing because of what you are, not to get something for yourself." We "inherit" the kingdom, Jesus says here. There's no such thing as "earning an inheritance." We come to the goal God wants for everyone by realizing that we're the sons and daughters of gift-love itself! We don't do these things described in the parable to earn

God's love. We do them finally because that is who we are—it's our true nature to give such love.

Visiting a hospital the other day, I saw a beautiful little girl running ahead of her parents down the hall. Somehow she fell and cut her chin open as she hit a flower pot on the way down. She immediately began to cry in great anguish. Three of us who were actually closer to her than her parents instinctively stooped over to do what we could to help. Her parents came right behind, of course, and took her to get the wound sewn up. My point is, the instinct to help that stricken child came perfectly naturally because there was no overlay of fear or prejudice. This is the way we humans act in the face of need when our true natures are at work. Gift-love is our birthright if only we knew it.

Look now at those on the left hand, however, whom Jesus described in very different terms. They confronted the same conditions as those on the right, yet they chose to do nothing. The hungry, the thirsty, the naked, the sick, the imprisoned—they were indifferent to them. Why? Here's the reality of need-love at work. These individuals whom Jesus described had nothing to give in terms of value or appeal, and therefore, no interest was shown in them. The true nature of those on the left came out when Jesus said, "I was hungry, and you gave Me nothing to eat, thirsty and you gave Me nothing to drink," and so forth. These folk were aghast. They asked, "When, O Mighty One, did we see You in need and passed up a chance to manipulate You and get in good with You? Had we known the King of the Universe was near, you can bet your last dollar we would have done something." But that's just the point—they were still stuck in need-love, and that represents where we start in the human saga, but not where we're suppose to end. This sort of self-serving behavior is literally "falling short of the glory," which is how St. Paul defines the essence of sin. The old Hebrew image is that of "missing the mark," of not yet being what we have it in us to be.

Now the whole point of Jesus giving us the final exam in the middle of the course isn't to frighten us into failure, but to inspire us to recognize and then began to actualize our true identities. We humans do what we do because at a deeper level we perceive who we are. The purpose of this parable isn't to get us to contrive a lot of humanitarian acts in order selfishly to acquire salvation. If you start feeding the hungry and clothing the naked simply to gain a reward, you've missed the whole point of this parable. What Jesus came to do was change the way we understand ourselves and our relationship to God, and the most important truth of all is this: God's love is gift-love, not need-love, and we're made in that image. There's an artesian well in everyone rooted in the abundance of God. All of us have royal blood coursing through our veins. We are what we are because of who our Parent is, and once this fact of identity gets deeply rooted in our being, then this kind of unself-conscious giving of self will become a way of life. This is another way of saying that we "inherit the kingdom prepared for us from the foundations of the world."

The proper application of this parable, then, is to ask, "Where am I on this continuum of need-love and gift-love? Am I still mired down in the illusion of not-enoughness, and therefore seeking to use everyone in sight to fill my emptiness?" That's why those on the left paid no attention to the needy ones—they were fixated on their own emptiness and were using all their energies to acquire for themselves. The truth of the matter is that such self-concern is unnecessary. We already are fulfilled if we only realized it, not by virtue of what we have to make of ourselves, but by virtue of what God has already made of us. All that we need has already been deposited in us by the grace of creation. Therefore, the kind of behavior that evoked Jesus's praise, "I was hungry and you gave Me to eat, I was thirsty and you gave Me to drink" isn't some kind of manipulative ploy. This parable is about identity, finally, and not surface behavior.

There's a medieval fable about a mother tiger who died giving birth to a cub. This meant the newly-born creature was without any support as it wandered through the forest. A pack of goats came upon the little tiger and sensing its plight, invited it to join their company. As the months went by, this creature gradually took on all the qualities of goatness, even though he was by nature a tiger.

One day the King Tiger, happening through the same forest, saw the tiger cub acting like a silly goat and roared out, "What's the meaning of this unseemly masquerade? Why are you behaving in such a way?" All the cub knew to do was to bleat nervously and begin to nibble grass. Then it dawned on the King Tiger what the problem was: This little creature had no idea who he was!

The older animal took the little one down to a river and let him see for the first time a reflection of himself. "See," the King Tiger said. "You're not really a goat, you're one of us." Then he laid back his head and let the creature hear how a tiger was suppose to sound. At that juncture, the King Tiger said, "Follow me, little one, and I'll teach you to become the grand thing you already are and possess in you to become."

This fable allegedly inspired T.S. Eliot to refer once to "Christ, The Tiger." Is there any wonder? Jesus did come as the embodiment of all that God ever intended human beings to be. "Follow Me, and I'll enable you to become the same grand thing!" That's what this parable is finally about. By showing us our true natures, Jesus opens the way for our becoming just that.

Where, then, are you on this continuum of becoming? Gift-love is your inheritance. Why not claim it now joyfully?

# 5

# The Petulant Children

*Luke 7:31-35*

*To what then shall I compare the men of this generation, and what are they like? They are like children sitting in the market place and calling to one another,*

> *"We piped to you, and you did not dance;*
> *We wailed, and you did not weep."*

—

For John the Baptist has come eating no bread and drinking no wine; and you say, 'He has a demon.' The Son of man has come eating and drinking; and you say, 'Behold, a glutton and a drunkard, a friend of tax collectors and sinners!' Yet wisdom is justified by all her children."

The setting of this story is that of a typical Palestinian village in the days of Jesus; namely, an open square with children playing noisily in every direction. To this day, children of that region have the run of the whole town. As there was very little privacy or comfort in individual homes, so the public space was where most of the waking hours were spent.

Kenneth Bailey served for many years as a missionary to Lebanon. This exposure gives him unusual insight into the details of so many of the parables. For example, in commenting on the parable of the prodigal son, Bailey makes much of the fact that although the younger son was still "a far way off," his old father saw him and "ran to meet him and embraced him." Bailey claims he did this to protect the returning son from the children of the village, who ran in packs and would have been quick to taunt and badger. They'd have wanted to know why he was dressed so shabbily and what happened to all the arrogant boasts he had made as he left.

These same children, however, are now the primary focus in this story. Every parent or teacher will quickly recognize the dynamics Jesus described here. In any gathering of children, there are usually two distinct groups—"the proposers" and "the reactors." To the question "What shall we do?" there are always the idea persons who come up with specific suggestions. In this parable, the first proposal was "Let's play wedding. Let's dress up in our parents clothes and act like we're getting married. Then, after the ceremony, we can have a feast and dance and imitate all the joyful things we've seen our parents doing." In that sparse and hard culture, weddings were the happiest of all occasions. For a blessed interval, the peasants could lay down their tools and let themselves go in the feasting and merrymaking.

If you've seen the musical *Fiddler on the Roof*, you may remember the incredible exuberance that characterized the wedding of Tevye's first daughter. So, the proposers said, "Let's play wedding and imitate the joy of the adults," but "the reactors" said, "We don't want to play wedding. We don't feel like it. We don't want to do happy things right now. We're not in the mood." The proposers, however, prove to be quite adaptable and flexible. Today we might classify them as co-dependents; that is, folk who are totally tuned in to what others want. One wag has said, "When a co-dependent is drowning, another person's life flashes before his eyes." They may not know what they feel, but they're very aware of what others feel and want. Thus, when the reactors say, "We don't feel like playing wedding," the proposers say, "Okay, so you're feeling bad, let's go with where you are. Let's play funeral. Let's imagine that some-one has died. We've seen how the big people wail, scream, and dress in black. If you're feeling as bad as you say you are, then let's play funeral and act like the worst has happened."

If a wedding was the high point of joy in Palestinian culture, the funeral experience was locat-ed at the opposite end of the scale; it was a season of great heaviness and mourning. Here you have the two extremes in human experience. Lo and behold, the same children who don't want to play wedding say testily, "No, we don't want to play funeral either. That isn't appealing to us." At this point, the pro-posers cease to be codependent and say in despair, "What is it with you people? We piped, and you didn't want to dance. We wailed, and you didn't weep. For God's sake, what do you want to do?"

What Jesus is mirroring here is one of the deepest problems in all human life; namely, a spirit of chronic dissatisfaction, no matter what one's circumstances may be. The Transactional Analysis people used to have a game called "Yes, But," which meant that whatever is proposed is promptly rejected out of hand. Here, in the image of hordes of petulant children, Jesus raises up an issue of towering significance for us all. It has both a historical and a personal dimension.

First of all, Jesus uses this story to describe where He was in the unfolding of His own career. You may remember that Jesus experienced resounding success when He first began His ministry. People flocked to Him by the hundreds. But then, as time went on, the kind of chronic dissatisfaction that characterized these children began to surface; criticism of who He was and how He lived His life began to mount. At this stage He told the parable of the sower and the various kinds of soils—how some seed fell on rocks or on shallow soil or among thorns. It was His way of coming to terms with failure and rejection. He was learning that three out of every four things He wanted to do wouldn't come to actualization, due to factors beyond His control.

This little parable reflects the same sort of realism on Jesus's part. He describes in pictorial language what was happening right before His eyes. You see, in that very era of history, God had launched a powerful initiative to bring redemption to His world. The two chief figures in this movement were actually cousins, John the Baptist and Jesus. In many ways, these two were quite different in how they went about their work.

They illustrate the two forms of change strategies that have been tried across the centuries to take bad situations and make them better. One is called "the revolutionary approach." Here you attack a problem from the outside. You dramatize the difficulty by having someone who isn't immersed in it come and say clearly, "Here's what's wrong here and here's what you have to do if you're going to change and survive." The folk who do this are called "radicals," and they usually promise all kinds of doom if something isn't done.

Back in the '60s, we had several such radicals in our culture, and John the Baptist was the embodiment in Jesus's day of this approach to personal and social change. He stands in the tradition of the Old Testament prophets. His insights were clear, and he had abundant courage. John was willing to stand up to anyone. He stated quite forthrightly that if things didn't change soon, terrible consequences were sure to occur.

John was the consummate outsider. He dressed in very sparse, desert fashion, and wouldn't eat anything but locusts and wild honey. He didn't touch any kind of strong drink and was very confrontational in the way he related to culture. What happens to most revolutionary prophets happened to John the Baptist. At first, he created quite a stir, but he so frightened people by his dire predictions that they began to regard him as crazy or totally out of touch with reality. He was finally arrested by the authorities and beheaded down on the shores of the Dead Sea.

On the other hand, Jesus came as a very different sort of change agent. He was more evolutionary than revolutionary. He chose initially to identify with people and connect up with their concerns, rather than to set himself over against them. His approach was to breathe new life on slumbering embers, to take the good that was already there and find a way to make it grow. This is a very different approach than the one of the radical who comes in with fire in his eyes and says, "Unless you change, terrible things are going to happen to you." This kind of change agent starts by coming close with tears in his eyes, not fire. He says "we" instead of "you" about the problem. He dares to get down where his own hands become dirty, where he suffers what other people are suffering, and from that stance within, he seeks to call forth the best and to cast out the worse.

This is the way that Jesus went about the redemptive task. First of all He identified himself with the people whom He was trying to save. He became what the people were so that they might become what He was. He ate what they ate, drank what they drank, and dressed like they dressed. He loved a good party. One of the first times we see Him in John's Gospel He's present at a wedding feast. He even bails out the embarrassed host by turning some water into wine. He was the joyous life of every party He ever attended and was known to all for His convivial spirit.

So what did the people of that day say of this One who chose to work from within rather than without? Well, they rejected Him with the same kind of chronic negativism that the petulant children displayed. When He started out, the common people heard Him gladly. He proceeded to love each one He ever met as if there were none other in all the world to love, and He loved all as He loved each. He excluded no one from the circle of His affection, and came to be known as "the Bridegroom of the World." Jesus identified with the least and the last and the worst, and what happened? The very same people who had rejected John the Baptist for being too negative and too austere rejected Jesus for being too loving and too lax! The very people who had said "John is crazy in his idealism," then said of Jesus, "He's no better than all the rest. Why, He is a friend of sinners. I saw Him eating the other day at table with some tax collectors. He is a wine bibber and a glutton. There's no difference between Him and the worst people in society."

In the experience of those who originally heard these words, two very different approaches to redeeming the world had been tried, and the people of that era wound up rejecting them both! Therefore, the little story about the petulant children was first of all a description of that moment in history, and how the best God had to offer was to offer wasn't enough, because of the negative mind-set of the very people Jesus came to save.

This parable says a lot about the conditions of that particular era in history, but there's another whole side to this issue. How does this apply to us and our attitudes, and how do we handle the ways God is trying to save us? It would be easy to point accusing fingers and say, "Can you imagine people having the benefit of somebody as wise as John the Baptist and not learning from him? Can you imagine people experiencing the love of Jesus and not letting that nurture them back to wholeness? Isn't it incredible how the people of that day were so out of it?"

Such an approach would miss the main point of this parable. This chronic condition of dissatisfaction—not really liking anything—is a basic problem with many of us. This is the depth of darkness in the human condition that Jesus came to confront, the wound that Jesus most wants to touch and to heal. In fact, I see this spirit of chronic dissatisfaction as the essence of sin and the polar opposite of what Holy Scripture says to us about the nature of God.

I've referred time and time again to the story in Genesis of how the One who had life in Himself decided to share that life with others. God's aliveness was something too good to keep to Himself. God wanted others to taste His form of ecstasy, which consisted of freely choosing to create, effectively carrying through on that resolve, and finally looking with delight on what He had done. The one thing you don't find anywhere in Genesis is a note of dissatisfaction. God didn't create out of some unhappy need in Himself that He was trying selfishly to fill, nor was He displeased with the outcome of His efforts. God's evaluation of the whole process is summed up in that exuberant refrain: "It's good! It's good! It's very, very good!"

Now obviously, something had occurred between that moment and what Jesus described as happening among those children in the village square. From whence did this utterly different attitude toward reality come? The Bible suggests that this is the bitter fruit of evil entering our human experience. Scott Peck notes our English word *evil* is *live* spelled backward; that's a cogent definition of this reality indeed. The opposite of what God intended is precisely what the petulant children represent.

If we were to put this problem in contemporary psychological terms, we would call it *neurotic negativism.* Karen Horney is widely recognized as one of the pioneer researchers in this area. She makes a simple distinction between two terms that are often confused; namely, *psychotic* and *neurotic.* A psychotic person, she affirms, is one who says, "Two plus two is five"; that is, they're out of touch with reality altogether. A neurotic, however, is one who says, "Two plus two is four, but I don't like it!" In other words, these individuals are in touch with reality, but it doesn't please them at all. This sort of person is a realist, all right, but a disgruntled and unhappy one.

There's a telling story about an English family who went on a picnic one day by the side of a beautiful lake. At one point their three-year-old son accidentally fell into the water; none of the adults in the family knew how to swim. Here was the child, bobbing up and down in the water and screaming for help, and here was the family jumping up and down on the bank in near hysteria. A man who happened to be passing by quickly sized up the situation, and at great risk to his own safety, dove into the lake, rescuing the lad before he sank for the final time. He climbed out on the bank with the child, who was badly frightened but basically all right, only to hear the mother ask testily: "Where's Johnny's cap?"

Let me suggest that this is classic neurotic behavior, the decision not to be happy no matter what the circumstances. We need to get in touch with the degree to which this way of seeing life is buried deeply in our own psyche. This is a problem that goes all the way back to what Genesis said happened to the whole race; that is, our earliest forebears bought into the serpent's lie about the nature of God.

More personally, however, this way of seeing life goes back to the perception of our own beginnings, according to Karen Horney. She traces the roots of neuroticism to what she calls "basic anxiety about one's self." And where does that come from? Again, she suggests that it goes back to the first thing that God ever did for us; namely, our creation or birth. If that event is regarded as something negative—that is, if one is dissatisfied with the body one has been given, with the mind one has, with the family system into which one was born, with the era of history in which one finds oneself—then it follows rather consistently that everything after birth will appear negative as well. This is the poison spring from which all neurotic feelings and behavior flow.

It reminds me of a continuum I saw years ago during the era when Transactional Analysis was so popular in our culture. The leader of a seminar I was attending drew a long diagram on the black board that contained a center and then five positions in either direction. He labeled one side +1, +2, +3, +4, +5, and the same numerals in a negative sequence in the other direction. These positions were defined this way. +1 stood for "I'm OK"; +2, "You're OK"; +3, "We're OK"; +4, "They're OK"; and +5, "It's OK." The negative sequence had the same pattern, only it read "I'm not OK," "You're not OK," "We're not OK," "They're not OK," and "It's not OK." The leader then designated the center point as the event of birth, and said that the way one chose to image that particular event set the tone for how one perceived everything else.

If I regarded the first thing that God ever did to

me as something good, then all the individuals and in-groups and out-groups and the whole of reality would be regarded positively as well. But if I chose to look on my birth event as something negative, the shadow of that initial displeasure would eventually swallow up everything else, and all that I subsequently encountered would be evaluated negatively.

This assertion reminded me of a seminary class years before when a professor said that Jesus's words about "loving our neighbors as ourselves" were a psychological principle as well as an ethical challenge. I'll never forget his saying forcefully, "You will love your neighbors as you love yourself. The way you choose to perceive the first person you encounter in history—namely, yourself—will lay down the tracks, so to speak, for all the other relationships that follow."

This ties in exactly with Karen Horney's contention, for what is "basic anxiety about one's self" but the decision to regard negatively the beginning point of our life in history? You see, if our original forebears had trusted the goodness of their own creation and been able to say from the start, "I really am OK as I came from the hand of God," then the serpent's suggestion that they become like gods would have never taken root. They could have replied: "We don't want to be gods. Being human is good enough in itself."

The basic anxiety about their worth opened the door to the suspicion that they were in fact "not

OK." That's how the whole human race got started in the wrong direction.

Some time ago I came across this quotation from a book entitled *Concepts of Personality* that sums up the effects of the fall quite graphically: "A sense of security is only possible if one is sure of his place, sure of his ability to cope with whatever may come, and sure of his worth and value. Anyone who believes he must energetically seek his place will never find it. He does not know that by his mere presence he already does belong and has a place. If one has to be more than he is in order to be somebody, he will never be anybody. If one doesn't realize that he's good enough as he is, he'll never have any reason to assume he's good enough, regardless of how much money, power, or superiority he may amass. Few people believe they're good enough as they are, and therefore can be sure of their esteemed place. Therefore, everyone is trying to be more, to be better, to reach higher. As a consequence, we are all neurotic in a neurotic society that pays a premium to the overly ambitious search for prestige and superiority. Underneath, we are all frightened people, not sure of ourselves, not sure of our worth, not sure of our place. It is this doubt of one's self, expressed in feelings of inadequacy and inferiority, which lies at the root of all maladjustment and all psychopathology."

This is precisely the condition from which Jesus came into the world to save us. To be released from such discontent represents redemption in its most profound form, and involves going all the way down and all the way back to the very first thing that ever happened to us and changing the way we choose to perceive that event. We need to regard our own creation the way God regards all creation; namely, as something "very, very good." This and this alone is the answer to the problem of "basic anxiety about one's self."

Agnes Stanford was the first person to introduce me to the intriguing concept of the "healing of the memories." She declares that the Risen Christ is no more bounded by time than He is by space. One of the effects of the Resurrection is that now Jesus has access to every facet of creation—past, present and future—as well as all places and spaces. What that means is that mercy now has a potency that it never had before. The Risen Lord is now able to go with us back down the corridor of our memories and stop at each place of woundedness and heal them as surely as He healed the lame and the blind during His earthly ministry.

Jesus can't change the shape of the past, for there is a has-finality to yesterday that cannot be altered. However, He can change the meaning of those events. They need no longer pour poison into our psyches, but by the grace of His healing touch, they can become springs of grace and wonder as we shift from thinking how bad we were to how good God is in being willing to forgive. The deepest dimension of this "healing of the memories" goes all the way back to our birth and transforms our perceptions of that event from something bad into something good.

Such an interpretation gives a new perspective to this term of *being born again.* At least part of what it means is that Jesus gives us a new way of reperceiving the event of our own beginnings and thus the whole of our lives. Then we, too, can begin to look on our creation the way Genesis depicts God as looking on all creation. When that begins to occur, then delight rather than dissatisfaction becomes the lens through which all is perceived. This movement from "I'm OK" then proceeds to include the individuals and in-groups and out-groups and finally all reality in a positive perspective. What begins with a new understanding of our own birth finally extends to the world itself, which means that the spirit of the petulant children, which is the essence of sin, is replaced by the spirit of the One who first looked on creation and pronounced it "good."

Sam Keen was raised in a little town in east Tennessee where his father taught in a small Presbyterian college. He claims that from the first he was engulfed by a sense of nobodiness—the feeling that as he was, he wasn't good enough. Like most American males of his era, he decided he had to go outside himself and import some significance to fill the emptiness within. Not surprisingly, academic achievement became his way of "trying to make something of himself." He did exceptionally well in school; on graduation from high school, he was accepted into Harvard University. He had always thought that if he could ever accomplish something like that, then his sense of nobodiness would evaporate and he would experience positive self-esteem. He had not been in Harvard long, however, before the feelings of elation left; he was back into having to prove his worth once more by what he accomplished. He managed, once again, to do well, and went on from Harvard to Princeton to work on a Ph.D. Alas, the satisfaction he had felt at graduating with honors turned out to be like "cotton candy"—a brief moment of sweetness, then nothing but emptiness in the mouth.

As Keen finished up at Princeton, he began to think that if ever he could get a job teaching and manage to publish a book, then a sense of well-being would finally be his. He proceeded to do both of these things, only to discover that he still was dominated by this sense of nobodiness. It all came to a climax when he was invited to give a paper at one of the learned academic societies that meet during the Christmas holidays. He had dreamed of doing this, but after the experience, he felt as empty as ever. He reports going back to his hotel room in Manhattan and getting down on his knees and crying out, "What must I do to be saved? How on earth can I find a sense of worth in the depths of my being?" He claims that as he cried out his despair, across the room, on the hotel wall, these words began to take shape. "Nothing! Nothing at all! It comes with the territory." At that moment he recalled the old image of a person "riding on an ox, and looking for an ox." Here was someone searching everywhere for reality, and all along it was there underneath him, but he had never seen it before!

This is what Jesus came to reveal to every one of us. By the grace of God, we are what we are. Our worth was put into us at creation. The secret of our life in Christ isn't getting something outside inside by achieving; the secret is recognizing what's already inside by the grace of creation, and learning to get this outside by sharing and serving. Thomas Merton calls this "the breakthrough to the Already"; it consists of seeing the first thing that ever happened to us—our birth—the way God sees it, and regarding it with Him as something "very, very good!"

This is the only antidote I know to the spirit of chronic dissatisfaction that characterized those children in Jesus's story. We can spend the rest of our lives asking "Where's Johnny's cap?" unless we allow the Risen Lord to take us all the way down and all the way back and truly reperceive the event of our birth. This is the beginning of seeing all things anew and aright, and also the beginning of grateful and joyful living!

# 6

# Love, Fear, and Our Neighbor

### *Luke 10:25-39*

*And behold, a lawyer stood up to put him to the test, saying, "Teacher, what shall I do to inherit eternal life?" He said to him, "What is written in the law? How do you read it?" And He answered, "You shall love the Lord your God with all your heart, and with all your soul, and with all your strength, and with all your mind; and your neighbor as yourself." And he said to him, "You have answered right; do this, and you will live."*

*But he, desiring to justify himself, said to Jesus, "And who is my neighbor?" Jesus replied, "A man was going down from Jerusalem to Jericho, and he fell among robbers, who stripped him and beat him, and departed, leaving him half dead. Now by chance a priest was going down that road; and when he saw him he passed by on the other side. So likewise a Levite, when he came to the place and saw him, passed by on the other side. But a Samaritan, as he journeyed, came to where he was; and when he saw him, he had compassion, and went to him and bound up his wounds, pouring on oil and wine; then he set him on his own beast and brought him to an inn, and took care of him. And the next day*

*he took out two denarii and gave them to the innkeeper,
saying, 'Take care of him; and whatever more you
spend, I will repay you when I come back.' Which of
these three, do you think, proved neighbor to the man
who fell among the robbers?" He said, "The one who
showed mercy on him." And Jesus said to him, "Go and
do likewise."*

—

Parables were often Jesus's way of diffusing con-
flictual situations and inserting surprising insights
that shifted the whole balance of perspective. This is
the case with the most famous of all the stories he
told—the one about the legendary Good Samaritan.

It begins with a lawyer asking Jesus a question, a
perennial question really. "What is life all about any-
way?" Sometimes we put the issue this way. "What
must I do to be saved?" At other times we ask, "How
can I find my highest fulfillment?" or "What is the
real reason for my existence?" This issue has been
phrased in a variety of ways, and represents a curiosi-
ty that is well-nigh universal. Who hasn't at times
wondered what is involved in getting in touch with
what is deepest and highest and most important in
all existence?

Jesus responded to the lawyer the way any first-
century rabbi would have done. "What is written in
the Law? How do you read it?" This was vintage
rabbinical procedure. I once asked a Jewish friend of
mine why people of his faith usually answer a question by asking another one? He got a wry smile on

his face and replied, "Why not?" There is, of course, profound wisdom behind such a practice.

Jesus realized that most people are not just empty vessels into which one pours answers directly. If a truth is going to make any difference in a person's life, it's going to have to connect up with where that person is already. Therefore, answering an inquiry by a further question is a way of probing the questioner more deeply, finding out exactly where they're coming from, and getting them involved in finding the answer they're seeking. This is a sound approach to authentic growth, indeed, and this is what Jesus did with the lawyer.

He answered in words the Hebrew people had used for centuries in expressing their faith. "You shall love the Lord your God with all of your heart, with all your soul, with all your strength, and with all your mind, and your neighbor as yourself." You'll find these very words again and again throughout the Old Testament. They represent the Jewish vision of reality at its best, and since this is the foundation to all that Jesus taught, let me underline just how seminal these words are.

In the biblical perspective, there are only two orders of reality: the uncreated, which has life in itself, and the created, which derives its life from the other. This is what we might call "contingent reality." It "hangs" like a chandelier. It's because Something Else has given it the right to be and caused it to be. There are, then, these two orders of reality. Nothing but God belongs on the Uncreated side of the line, and everything except God belongs on the created side. Meister Eckehart put it succinctly once when he wrote, "It's God's nature to give being. It's creation's nature to receive being."

Once you get this fundamental distinction clear, it isn't surprising to find that we're to relate to the two orders in radically different ways. For example, we're to relate to the uncreated—the already perfect and complete—by loving "with all our hearts and minds and souls and strength"; that is, we're to assume a stance of worship toward that on which we ultimately depend. We're to set that One in a category all by himself, because there's nothing—absolutely nothing—exactly like him. He is the Lord our God and Something to be distinguished from all other realities. We're invited to love everything else on the created side of the line the way a parent loves a child, or the way a gardener would love the seed that he carefully husbands to its fulfillment. Everything that derives its life from Another is to be nurtured; only the Lord God is to be worshipped and recognized as an Absolute.

If you and I can get the distinction between these two realities clear in our minds and learn to relate appropriately to each of them, this would be "the secret of eternal life," and the key to fulfilling the destiny that was intended for us.

Our great problem here, however, is the issue of idolatry; that is, taking something that is on the created side of the line, and relating to it as if it were the Uncreated. Whenever we take something that isn't God and relate to it in a worshipful stance; that is, expect from it everything that we humans need, such behavior leads to profound disillusionment. St. Augustine once prayed, "Thou hast made us for thyself, O God, and our hearts are restless until they rest in thee."

Mark it down that just as you can never get milk from a statue or wine from a stone, you can't get your ultimate fulfillment from anything save your divine Source. Whatever on the created side of the line is elevated to a place of worship—be that a child, a job, or a possession—is going to leave one profoundly unfulfilled. It doesn't have in it that for which our hearts ultimately hunger. We were made to live worshipfully toward the uncreated alone. We're never told to love our children "with all our hearts and minds and souls and strength." We're never told to love our parents or anything else, for that matter, in this way. Only God is to be revered absolutely; everything else is to be loved in those forms of nurture that encourage the creature to become what it has in it to be. God is already complete and is to be loved accordingly, while everything else is in the process of being completed, and thus all Jesus's teachings rest on this ancient understanding of reality. Although the Bible does not use the image of "a plan of salvation," this would be it, should you decide to formulate one: "You shall love the Lord your God with all your heart, soul, and strength, and love your neighbor as yourself."

I remember years ago I had a young parishioner who went away to college. He was like so many in that he had been taught the faith all his life, but was really not that interested in it. When he got to college, however, he encountered an intense group of fundamentalists and had a profound religious experience of his own. He came back literally "with fire in his eyes," saying "Why haven't I ever heard the Gospel before? My parents and my church don't know anything about the Lord." He felt he was absolutely superior to everybody else because of his newfound experience.

I've seen many adolescents go through this phase. I always celebrate what they've discovered and am patient with their accusations. I know that as they continue into the Way, things are not going to stay as simple as they appear to them in those beginning moments. I knew the college freshman was going to need me later on, and sure enough, six months later he was back in my study in great distress.

"I've been reading the Bible a lot lately," he told me. "This group that I'm with says there's only one way—a single plan for salvation; but I can't find it as I read the Scriptures. Jesus talks out of all sides of his mouth, it seems. For example, Nicodemus came to him to ask what he must do to be saved, and Jesus told him that he had to be born again. But when the woman by the well in Samaria encountered Jesus, he told her she needed to drink of the living water that would quench her thirst in an ultimate way. And when the rich young ruler comes with the same desire and the same question, Jesus doesn't say anything about being born again or drinking living water, but instead commands him to go and sell what he has, give it away to the poor, and follow him. Where's the one plan of salvation?"

"That's a very good question," I replied. "What you need to realize is that there's a common foundation underneath all these prescriptions. Jesus was like any good physician. He didn't prescribe the same medicine for every patient who walked through the door. He proportioned the medication to the particular sickness he detected. The one plan of salvation is this. 'You shall love the Lord your God with all your heart, mind, soul and strength.' Yet this had to be applied to the idolatries of each individual. For example, Nicodemus was a Jewish leader, a person who probably prized above all else that he had been born into this world a physical descendant of Abraham. This meant more to him than anything else. He had taken something on the created side of the line and was treating it as the uncreated, which is why Jesus challenged him as he did: 'You need to reperceive this matter of being born all over again. It's the fact that you're a son of God, not a son of Abraham that ought to matter most.' When it came to the Samaritan woman, however, the shape of her idolatry was quite different. She had made sensuality and feeling the central issue in life, which meant she needed to experience God as the Source of her delight, not anything on the created realm. The rich young ruler, on the other hand, didn't worship his Jewishnesss nor sensuality. It was his material possessions that had gotten over on the uncreated side of the line. This is why Jesus said to him that he needed to give away that on which he had come to depend and begin to trust the Maker of all things. This one had confused the means by which he lived for the End for whom he should live. Jesus invited him to shift his ultimate allegiance."

I tried to help this lad see that there was a single plan of salvation, but it had to be applied to the shape of each one's particular idolatry. If you comb the Gospels carefully, Jesus talked about the first law of Moses more than all the other nine put together. We're to have no other gods before the only God there is; or to put it another way, we're to love our Source as we love nothing else, and to love the rest of creation with the kind of nurturing affection that enables it to grow. Therefore, when Jesus heard the lawyer formulate the classic Hebrew vision, He applauded him. "You've got it! That's it in a nutshell. All you have to do is to put this vision into practice, and you'll inherit eternal life. The secret is yours. Go and live your life accordingly."

The lawyer, however, apparently had other things on his agenda beyond finding out truth for himself. After all, the passage says in the beginning that he was "putting Jesus to the test." Thus, after Jesus helped him to see that he already knew the answer to the question he was asking, the lawyer, instead of embracing that and going out to live it, attempted to save face by asking a further question. "Just a minute. Exactly who is my neighbor?"

I sense this lawyer was doing something here that I've often done myself. You see, I have two very different forms of needs. There are times in my life when I am so confused that I don't know how to put left foot in front of my right foot. What I need in those moments is some words of direction and guidance. There are other times, however, when I know exactly what I'm supposed to do, but I don't want to do it, or don't have the energy to do it, or somehow don't have the courage to put it into practice. And the truth is, I'm not above hiding behind the first to avoid the second, of spinning out complexities when in fact the issue is action and not confusion.

This is what I see the lawyer doing in this situation. It had really become clear what he was supposed to do. He was to love God in one way and the rest of creation in another. Yet, rather than putting his energies toward actualizing this ideal, he resorted to a delaying tactic and raised another complex issue. "Exactly who is my neighbor?" the man wanted to know.

The question has been debated in every age. How is the identity of a neighbor to be defined? He was really asking, "How far does my responsibility go here? What, in fact, constitutes neighborness, and who qualifies to receive the love called for in the Law?" He might have been asking, "What is the least I am required to do to get by?"

Laws evoke this kind of attitude. Like paying income tax, one wants to obey the law but doesn't want to pay one more cent than is required. At this point, Jesus realized, I think, that he was up against somebody who wasn't just seeking the truth. Here was a complex man with all kinds of issues at work at several levels of his life. And so, instead of giving him a direct answer, Jesus told him this parable.

When people heard Jesus say, "A certain man was going down from Jerusalem to Jericho," they knew this to be literally true. The city of Jerusalem is on the highest elevation in Palestine, some twenty-three hundred feet above sea level, while Jericho is down by the Dead Sea at the lowest place on this planet, some thirteen-hundred feet below sea level. Thus, in the span of a very few miles, there's a precipitous drop. The road was quite circuitous and narrow, with desert on either side. To this day, that road is known as the "Red and Bloody Way," because so much violence occurred there. The very thing Jesus described took place there all the time. It was easy for robbers to slip in from the desert, assault and rob somebody, and then disappear back into the desert. Therefore, this place and this kind of behavior were utterly familiar.

Thus, Jesus told of a man being robbed and left

half-dead, and then of three familiar figures passing by where the stricken man was lying. Each one of them would have been easily recognizable to a Palestinian audience. There was a Priest of the Temple, who represented religion at its professional best, a man who had been given the responsibility of not only presiding over the sacrifices but also of keeping alive the traditions of Israel. Second was a Levite, who was a lower-level Temple functionary; he too had the responsibility of carrying on the traditions of the Hebrews.

The third person making his way by this stricken person was identified as "a Samaritan." These were the racial half-breeds of first-century Palestine. Any time a Jewish person married a non-Jewish person and a child was born, that offspring was labeled a Samaritan. You don't need a doctorate in history to know that individuals of mixed racial heritage have an especially difficult time in any era with dominate groups. Do you remember those children from the Vietnam War who had African American fathers and Vietnamese mothers? The push to try to place these children in adoptive homes was met with great resistance. Historically, people with this form of origin are not accepted by any group. They wind up being rejected by almost everybody, occupying a kind of no-man's-land, which few will embrace.

This was the plight of first-century Samaritans. Because they were ostracized, they often lived up to this cultural expectation. Because they were so widely regarded as worthless, they acted as if they were worthless. Folk of that day wouldn't have expected anything humane, heroic or compassionate from a Samaritan; in fact, they probably would have surmised that a Samaritan would have gone over and tried to plunder the already beaten victim.

The most characteristic thing about a parable is the element of surprise. Jesus's story had the lawyer so enthralled that his defenses were down. Precisely at that moment, he shocked the life out of him by saying it was the Samaritan—not the priest or the Levite—who reacted humanely, even heroically, in that situation. He was the one to stop, go over to the stricken man, and do what he could to help him. He put him on his own beast of burden and took him to the nearest inn, which had facilities for long-term care and which he paid for out of his own pocket.

Here's an incredible example of loving a neighbor. It came from a person that no one in that society would have suspected. All the hearers, not just the lawyer, must have been astonished. Jesus asked, "Which one of these three proved neighbor to the man who was in need?" Once again, the answer was obvious—the one who showed pity. Then Jesus said, "Go and do likewise."

It's important to notice what Jesus did with that question, "Who is my neighbor?" He turned it around one hundred and eighty degrees and focused it on the lawyer, not on anyone else. There was a long tradition among the Hebrews of finding ways to

limit their liabilities. Again and again this term
"neighbor" was trimmed to smaller and smaller pro-
portions; for example, only those who were descend-
ed from Abraham or who had property were considered neighbors.

Jesus, however, turned in the other direction altogether and said, "You're to think of yourself as a
neighbor." The question isn't, "Is such and such a person worthy of my love?" but rather, "Am I willing to
take what I have, what I know, and what I can do
and place all this at the disposal of another person's
needs or growth?"

Before there was anything except this Mystery,
God said, "This is too good to keep. I want others
to get in on what I am and what I am experiencing.
I want to share the wonder of My aliveness with creatures in My own images." Remember, according to
the Bible, creation comes out of God's generosity.
We humans are made in that image! Thus, what the
Samaritan did on the Jericho road was to act out
what it means to be made in the image of primal
generosity. Loving one's neighbor is making a gift of
what we've been given by God. "Loving our neighbors as ourselves" answers to the deepest impulses
within us. We love because it's our nature to love.
We don't ask, "Are they worthy?" but rather, "Am I
willing to act out the image of God that is within?"

What keeps us from acting out of our highest and
best? In terms of the parable, why was it the
Samaritan, not the priest and Levite, who stopped to

help the stricken man? Let's ponder the dynamics of our own hearts as we ask this probing question.

It could be a question of courage. The priest and Levite may have allowed fear to dehumanize them. They had an innate sense of compassion, like everyone else, but when they saw the beaten man and realized where they were—the Red and Bloody Way—all their high ideals and religious motivations evaporated. Fear does cast out love. It contracts our vision to ourselves and ourselves alone. Perhaps this fear accounts for otherwise good men deciding to do nothing except run for their own lives. The Samaritan, on the other hand, might have been in touch with the Reality that is greater than fear, the Reality of Love. This is what enables a person to cast out fear and create courage. Paul Tillich used to claim that courage was the virtue foundational to all others, and that we're not likely to get very far in loving God, our neighbors, or ourselves unless we're empowered by it.

Then again, perhaps the three men acted differently on the Red and Bloody Way because of time pressure. Realize, if you will, that the priest and Levite might have had obligations at the Temple to fulfill. The Samaritan, on the other hand, might not have been so tightly committed. Thus, he had a freedom to respond spontaneously to the unexpected in ways that the highly structured priest and Levite couldn't.

I heard years ago of an interesting experiment that was conducted to ascertain what factors enabled people to act lovingly and what factors worked against the same thing. A seminary professor recruited fifteen volunteers from his class to meet him at his office at two P.M. When they arrived, he handed out sealed instructions.

Five of the envelopes instructed the recipients to proceed across the campus without delay. They were told, "You have fifteen minutes to reach this place. You have no time to spare. Don't loiter or do anything else, or your grade will be docked." These five were coded "The High Hurry Group."

The next five were instructed that, anytime in the next forty-five minutes, they were to make their way across the campus. "You've plenty of time," they were told, "but don't be too slow." They were coded "The Medium Hurry Group."

The last five were told that, any time before five o'clock that afternoon, they were to report across campus, and there they would receive further instructions. This group was known as "The Low Hurry Group."

Unbeknownst to any of these students, the professor had arranged with some drama majors at Princeton University to be situated alongside the path they had to take, simulating great human needfulness. One was sitting with his head in his hands, crying and wailing in a way one couldn't ignore. Another was lying face down, as if he had had some kind of seizure and was unconscious. Still another was shaking violently as if he were about to throw up. All fifteen of the students had to make their way past these obviously needy persons, and here's what happened.

None of "The High Hurry Group" stopped to see what they could do, although all five of them aspired to be Christian ministers. Two of "The Medium Hurry Group" stopped to try to help. All five of "The Low Hurry Group" made attempts to be responsive. The point that emerged out of all of this was that pressure is a moral category. Anytime we get ourselves overbooked or have too many irons in the fire, it affects our ability to respond to the unanticipated. No matter how lofty our idealism, when our date book is filled to the hilt, it shapes what we do.

This might well have been the problem for the priest and the Levite, while perhaps the Samaritan was more realistic. Maybe he had learned that his limits were as much a part of him as his gifts. What he couldn't do said as much about how God had made him as what he could do. Whether or not this was the reason, here's something for all of us to consider. Do our busy lives keep us from being what we really want to be? Raw evil isn't the only temptation most of us face. At times, the good can become an enemy of the best, especially when we take on too many "good causes" and forget our limits.

A third possibility here could have been an overly judgmental attitude on the part of the priest and Levite that the Samaritan simply didn't share.

Perhaps on seeing this beaten man, these two said to themselves, "He was foolish to have been traveling alone with items of value. Everybody knows that if you're carrying precious cargo, you need to travel this way in caravans, not by yourself." Therefore, they might have rationalized their way out of doing anything on the grounds that the victim deserved his fate because of his own foolishness. "He made his bed—now let him lie in it," they might have reasoned.

On the other hand, maybe the Samaritan was more immediate and less analytical in the way he saw the situation. His attitude might have been, "Need justifies ministry." He probably wouldn't have argued that we need to look into the reasons why bad things happen to people. Once a person is robbed and beaten and lying by the side of the road, elaborate speculation on how he got there is secondary to doing something about his wounds.

I once saw a sign that read, "Yes, I'd like to help you out. Show me how you came in." It smacks of evading help by resorting to analysis. There's a place for this sort of thing, but it ought to come after the oil and bandages and wine have been applied. Perhaps the Samaritan realized that we humans never know enough to judge another person absolutely, but we do know enough to take what we have and place it at the disposal of another's need. God never asks any of us to occupy the seat of judgment, but he does call us to wash each other's feet and do what we can to be of practical help. In doing this, which was certainly not all that needed to be done, the Samaritan was clearly superior to the two who decided to do nothing.

A fourth reason why it could have been the Samaritan and not the priest and Levite might have been that he alone had with him certain things that matched the needs of that moment. After all, Jesus did mention "oil and clothes and wine and a donkey," all of which the Samaritan readily shared. It's entirely possible, given their professions, that the priest and Levite carried none of these things with them. Thus, when they saw the man and realized his dire needs, they decided the best thing they could do was go as quickly as possible for help. If this is why they swiftly "passed by on the other side," I'd say their response was as loving as that of the Samaritan.

The point here is that we're never called on to give what we don't have, or expected to do things for people that we're not capable of doing. It's important to recognize that our response to people involves more than just their needs. The particular shape of our giftedness is a determinant as well. It would be irresponsible to rush into situations where we don't have the ability to be part of the answer. If you're having an attack of appendicitis, it would be criminal for me to try to resolve the problem. You need the services of a competent surgeon.

I was stopped at a red light some time ago, where I noticed a car on the other side of the busy thoroughfare; a middle-aged woman was helplessly looking under the hood. She was obviously stalled and didn't know what to do. I decided to try to help, but let me describe the form that helpfulness assumed. I don't know the first thing about auto mechanics; if I had gotten under that hood and tried to remedy the problem, I would have probably made it worse. So what I did was pull over and offer to go to a service station two blocks away.

When I suggested this, she beamed and said, "That would be wonderful."

"Is there anybody I can call for you?" I asked.

"Would you mind telephoning Rita at the Bon Ton Beauty Shop and tell her that my car is on the blink and I'm going to be late?" she replied.

Now, those were two things that I could do, and I proceeded to perform them with dispatch. Therefore, maybe the differential here had to do with hard practicalities. The Samaritan had with him what was needed; the priest and Levite didn't. If they hastened to get appropriate help, they were just as faithful as the Samaritan. We need to be careful, lest we make love look like doing the impossible. It really consists of doing what you can with what you have for the help or growth of another. You don't have to have a Ph.D. to love your neighbor.

The last possibility is that the Samaritan stopped because he was a Samaritan, and a very special one at that. Remember that Samaritans were racial half-breeds and roundly disliked by everybody. They didn't really belong anywhere. Given this special historical burden, they tended to respond to their destiny in one of three ways. Most Samaritans simply gave up in the face of all this hostility, crept to the sidelines, and lived out their days in quiet despair. The majority of Samaritans were deeply depressed people. A smaller group of Samaritans took the opposite approach. They were enraged at the injustice of treating persons this way for something over which they had no control. They became revolutionaries who attempted to strike out in anger at these unjust structures. They were ready to do whatever they could to overthrow the establishment. They were willing to resort to violence to give their oppressors a taste of their own medicine. But the trouble was, there were so few Samaritans in relation to the Jews and the Romans that whenever they turned to violence, they were the ones who wound up getting hurt.

There's a wonderful old Yiddish saying to the effect that when a chicken challenges an elephant to a fight, the chicken had better be agile. In other words, if a tiny amount of strength dares to provoke a great deal of bulk, the chicken had better know how to move and move fast! Well, the Samaritans were the chickens, the Romans and the Jews were the elephants; most of the time it was the Samaritans who were destroyed.

But there was yet a third group of Samaritans, the smallest in number, but the most admirable in their

approach. These were the Samaritans who took the
injustices of their experience in history and somehow
transmuted these into awareness and sensitivity to
other suffering people. They also developed a compassion that wanted to keep others from being hurt
as they had been hurt. It could be that the
Samaritan in Jesus's story was just such a special suf-
ferer. Here was a man who knew in his own experience what it was like to be "beaten and left by the
side of the road." He was no stranger personally to
this sort of harsh treatment. However, instead of giving up in despair or blowing up in rage, this man had
somehow transmuted his suffering into something
higher, which explains why he saw the man by the
side of the road, and was moved to help.

There's no way to prove that is the proper explanation, but to me it is the most heroic. Of all the
things that I would like to do with my days and
nights, I can think of nothing more appealing than
becoming one who chooses to take his wounds and
transpose them into awareness, sensitivity, and compassion. I don't think there are many persons who
have had the same kind of injustices perpetrated on
them as had the Samaritans, but if everyone of us
could tell our own story, we've all had things happen
to us that we can't understand. We've all lost people
whom we loved and tasted bitter disappointments.
We too have also been tempted to respond to these
hurts by giving up on life and becoming bitter and
angry people. But there's always this alternative—to

turn our wounds into the desire to bless and help—to become what Henri Nouwen calls "wounded healers." And, for me at least, there's no higher goal or aspiration.

I admit, then, there's no conclusive answer to the question of why it was the Samaritan and not the priest or the Levite who stopped and loved his bruised neighbor. It could have been many things, but the point is, the Samaritan did it, and so can we.

Go, then, and do likewise!

# 7

# A Midnight Request

*Luke 11:5-13*

The longer I live, the more convinced I become that there are only two basic realities—love and fear. At the functional level, love is the perception that we humans are created in the image of an abundant One, that what we already have is adequate to meet any crises we might confront. This sense of sufficiency is the source of what Charles Boddie used to call "cope-ability"—the courage to deal resourcefully with whatever occurs.

Fear, however, is at the opposite end of this continuum. It's the perception that there isn't enough and never will be—not enough knowledge, not enough power, not enough love. This means that one is always outmatched by reality—up against the overpowering—and such a perception does destructive things all the way around.

If it is true that love has the power to cast out fear, as the writer of the Epistle in 1 John affirms (4:18), it is equally true that fear has the power to cast out love. I'm never less loving than when I'm most afraid. Fear turns all of us into egocentric monsters, able to think of hardly anything but ourselves and prone either to all sorts of destructive behavior or complete indifference to the plight of others. Fear is the great unmaking of the highest and the best in human beings. This fact highlights the importance of learning to perceive reality in terms of abundance rather than scarcity.

What occurs on the perceptional level is what shapes our behavior. This is precisely where Jesus chose to do his redemptive work and why parables like this one of the neighbor's midnight request is of such seminal importance. It speaks directly to the issue of Ultimate Reality. What is the Mystery behind it all really like? To whom exactly do we address our prayers? In the following words, Jesus provides us a powerful and a hopeful answer.

—

*Which of you, who has a friend, will go to him at midnight and say to him: "Friend, lend me three loaves; for a friend of mine has arrived on a journey, and I've nothing to set before him"; and he will answer from within, "Don't bother me; the door is now shut, and my children are with me in bed; I can't get up and give you anything." I tell you, though he won't get up and give him anything because he is his friend, yet because of his importunity, he will rise and give him whatever he needs. And I tell you, ask and it will be given you; seek and you will find; knock and it will be opened to you. For everyone who asks receives, and he who seeks finds, and to him who knocks, it will be opened. What father among you, if your son asks for bread, will give him a* stone. *Or if he asks for a fish, will instead of a fish give him a serpent; or if he asks for an egg, will give him a scorpion? If you then, who are evil, know how to give good gifts to your children, how much more will the heavenly Father give the Holy Spirit to those who ask Him?*

—

Anyone, even a child, could understand Jesus. The details of this parable reflect very accurately the way first-century Galilean peasants lived. It needs to be remembered that back in those days, people traveled largely on foot. Because of the excessive heat, the accepted practice was to start out late in the afternoon and walk into the first part of the night. So, it wasn't at all unusual that at midnight, an unexpected relative might appear at the door asking for hospitality. One also needs to realize that there were very few public inns in that era, which is why hospitality was regarded as such a virtue. It was the only way that poor people could travel and survive.

Thus, many times, if a person had to make a journey, he would plot his course carefully in order to get to Cousin George's tonight and Aunt Sarah's tomorrow night. On the hosting end, it was common courtesy to give a weary traveler something to eat, no matter how late he arrived. That's precisely the context of Jesus's little story.

A friend arrived in the dead of the night; the host found himself without sufficient food. Peasants in that day lived very close to the edge. There was rarely much surplus of anything. Rather than embarrass himself, however, and send his guest to bed hungry, the host excuses himself, goes next door, and asks his neighbor if he could bail him out by giving him three loaves. These represented about what the average meal at that time would have been. The response of the man next door was utterly typical.

Again, one needs to realize that most peasant houses were one-room enclosures. Many of them didn't have windows. There was usually a single door that afforded access both inside and out, a dirt floor, some kind of stove against a wall, and pegs on which people could hang things. The cooking was done outside; in fact almost everything was done outside. The houses were basically sleeping places. After supper the father would gather up his tools and his animals and move them inside. Then he'd call in his wife and children and close the door. He'd bank the fire, put a bushel over the lamp to keep it from blowing out, and then they'd lie down together on the dirt floor, the children being closest to the stove. It would be totally dark inside.

The accepted courtesy was that you didn't bother a neighbor once the closing rituals of the day had occurred. This accounts for the initial response to the neighbor's request. A voice from within responded sleepily. "Can't you see that the door is shut? Don't you know that my children are in bed with me?" That was literally the case; they were all around him on the dirt floor, and it was utterly dark.

"I can't get up and give you bread at this time of night. It would wake up the world!"

I must pause at this point and acknowledge empathy for this poor man. I remember what it was like as a parent finally to get the children down for the night. I imagine little ones in every age have attempted to string out going to bed as long as possible. For example, my children developed incredible thirsts about nine o'clock each night, and an insatiable desire for stories.

My son, who is now in his thirties, was particularly skilled in extending this process. When I'd be absolutely worn out, he'd plead, "Tell me about Jesus." What was a minister to do? How can you turn your back on that kind of open door to religious instruction? It was all a ruse, of course, to keep things going as long as he could. The eleventh commandment at our house was: "Never wake a sleeping child!" There were no crises severe enough to justify starting the going-to-bed process all over again! Therefore, I feel for this drowsy neighbor—the canons of common courtesy had been violated.

The embarrassed host, however, wasn't willing to give up easily. He kept on knocking at the door until, I suppose, the children were awakened. By this time, the whole inside was a sea of turmoil; the neighbor, probably saying under his breath, "Anything to get rid of that loudmouth from next door," got up, took the bushel off the lamp, went to the cupboard, fetched what the neighbor was requesting, and sullenly handed it over. Persistence won out over reluctance; one man went home happy; another household was left in shambles.

This may have been the story Jesus told in response to the request, "Teach us to pray," but quite frankly, for years I have been troubled by the whole thing. The surface meaning seems to suggest that persistence is the key to authentic praying. If we keep at it long enough, we finally wear God out and God says, "Okay, okay, since I can't get rid of you in any other way, I'm going to give you what you're asking."

Such an image is hardly an appealing theological vision. It seems to reverse the Creator/creature relationship altogether, and give the pushiest among us the upper hand and the final say, which isn't reassuring at all. Thus, for a long period, this was a closed passage for me.

Then one day, someone pointed out to me a linguistic detail that shifted my whole perspective. It was that the common conjunction in Greek—*kai*—can be translated either "and" or "but," depending on the context. "And" links together things that are in continuity with each other, while "but" signals a shift in direction. "But" is an introduction to contrast, not continuation, and translating the conjunction at the center of this parable in this way gives the story a totally new twist. Hence, "he will rise and give him whatever he needs. But I tell you, ask and it will be given you...."

It suddenly dawned on me that this notion of persistence winning out over reluctance was the pagan notion of prayer, not the vision Jesus came to give. He was putting here in story form what fear had done to the human understanding of God. Hadn't the serpent in the Garden of Eden suggested that God wasn't good and couldn't be trusted? Hadn't he implied that there was finally not enough in the Holy One, so that life became "everyone for himself."

If you're at all conversant with the literature of paganism, you will realize how negative the assumptions were about the gods and their attitudes toward human beings. The hallmark of pagan divinities was their indifference to the human plight, even their downright hostility to the creatures of Earth. The great sadness in those parts of the world that have never been touched by the biblical story of a blessing God is rooted in the belief that at the bottom of reality, there's Something that either doesn't care for us at all, or if it does care, cares only in very negative ways.

One of the most famous pagan myths is about a lesser god named Prometheus. One day he looked down from Mount Olympus and saw human beings stumbling around in the dark and the cold. Somehow this situation evoked compassion in him. He took some fire from the altar of Heaven and brought it down to the human race that they might be illumined and warmed. When the king god, however, discovered what Prometheus had done, he was furious. Prometheus had violated one of the laws of Heaven, which was that no god should feel compassion for earth. Therefore, Prometheus was punished by being chained to a rock, with a vulture eating endlessly at his insides.

This is a metaphor for the deep aversion it was believed Heaven had for Earth. It puts into language the way paganism felt about the divine reality. What happened to humans simply didn't matter to the gods. In this sense, the awakened neighbor has no sympathy for this crisis of hospitality, is a graphic image of the pagan understanding of the gods. It also follows that the persistent wearing down another is the pagan understanding of prayer!

It would be a great mistake, however, to relegate such attitudes to ancient times and distant cultures. Unless you're very different from me, I dare say you'll find elements of this same sort of fearfulness deep inside you. For example, when you hear the term "the will of God," is your first reaction one of elation and intrigue, or apprehension and uneasiness? What do you honestly think would happen if you did turn your whole life over to God completely? Would things get better or worse than they are now?

I heard once of a little boy who was asked in Sunday School, "What do you think God is like?"

"God is the Great Killjoy. He always has a frown on his face as he walks around. If he finds anybody having a good time, he puts a stop to it as quickly as possible."

In all honesty, is such an image completely foreign to the way you feel at the deepest level? We may not voice such uneasiness openly, but my sense is that it lies buried in the subconscious of most of us. The apprehensions of paganism have been alive and well in me at times. And I don't think I am alone in this. Many people have acknowledged to me that they believe if they ever did open the door to God, he would promptly demand they give up everything they enjoy.

Let me suggest that this is precisely the place where Jesus came to do the work of reconciliation, and this parable is one of His instruments. For having given graphic expression to a fearful image of God, He spoke dramatically. "But I say to you, ask and it shall be given you, seek and you will find, knock and it will be opened to you." And then in poetic parallelism, he repeated those same truths. "Everyone who asks will receive, everyone who seeks will find, and to everyone who knocks, it will be opened."

By that contrast, Jesus set an utterly different image of God against the fears of ages. The neighbor wasn't a mirror image of the true God, but the antithesis of what this One is. And then to drive the point home, Jesus described the way a healthy parent responds to a child. "What father among you, if his son were to ask for a loaf of bread, would give him a stone instead? Or, if he were to ask for an egg, would hand him a scorpion to mock him?"

He went on. "If you, who are less than perfect, know how to do good gifts to your children, how much more will the Father in Heaven give the Holy Spirit to those who ask him?" You see, to the mystery of Goodness, Jesus gave a face, and on that face he put a smile—the expression of a loving Parent—which is another way of saying that Jesus ultimately opened the way for love to cast out fear and for a sense of sufficiency to take the place of longing.

When this happens at the deepest level, then prayer ceases to be a pressing of reluctance and becomes rather a confident sharing with One who already cares. This, of course, becomes the secret of the cope-ability of which I wrote earlier. One can face up to any and all eventualities if one's sense of the Ultimate One is that of abundance and adequacy.

I was privileged as a little child to be exposed to a human being in whom Jesus really had effected this shift from fearfulness to love. She was an old black lady named Gladys Meggs. She lived in our home for almost a decade and served our family in every way. I remember she was always cheerful and full of life. If you asked her why this was so, she'd make this answer. "Ain't nothin' going to happen today that me and Jesus can't handle!"

That's good theology, and precisely the sort of mind-set this little parable was meant to convey. We don't pray to One who slumbers in indifference. No, we pray to One who gives us more than we can ask or expect—God's very self in the Holy Spirit—

because that is God's nature as loving Parent.

There is, then, enough—always has been and always will be—and realizing this makes all the difference!

# 8

## The Rich Fool

### Luke 12:13-21

*One of the multitude said to him, "Teacher, bid my brother divide the inheritance with me." But he said to him, "Man, who made Me a judge or divider over you?" And He said to them, "Take heed, and beware of all covetousness; for a man's life does not consist in the abundance of his possessions." And he told them a parable, saying, "The land of a rich man brought forth plentifully; and he thought to himself, 'What shall I do, for I have nowhere to store my crops?' And he said, 'I will do this: I will pull down my barns, and build larger ones; and there I will store all my grain and my goods. And I will say to my soul, Soul, you have ample goods laid up for many years; take your ease, eat, drink, and be merry.' But God said to him, 'Fool! This night your soul is required of you; and the things you have prepared, whose will they be?' So is he who lays up treasure for himself and is not rich toward God."*

———

Peter deVries, a novelist who once considered becoming a minister himself, has written a funny novel in which one of the characters is a very liberal Unitarian minister who prides himself on being as abstract and esoteric as possible. He was particularly pleased with himself one Sunday when he began his sermon by saying, "It's an aspect of God's omnipotence that He can save us without having to exist."

If asked, I'd wager that none of the listeners that day had had any idea as to what that string of words meant! In contrast, if you look deeply at the stories of Jesus, you won't encounter the kind of verbal stuff that goes over one's head or in and out of one's ears. These parables invariably touch us where we live or hurt or experience some need.

Such a process occurs in the twelfth chapter of Luke's Gospel, where Jesus, teaching the multitudes, was suddenly interrupted by a man who was obviously quite upset. "Teacher, bid my brother divide the inheritance with me." Disputes about inheritances were very common in that time, for the social arrangement of the family dictated that the oldest son assumed control the moment his father died, acquiring the responsibility for settling the estate with all the other siblings.

In Jesus's story of the prodigal son, the older brother probably got a two-thirds share, simply by virtue of his birth order, while the prodigal got only one-third. If there were more than two children, the oldest son probably would have received one half of the estate; everybody else would have received a portion of what was left. The point was that first-born sons occupied exceedingly powerful positions in ancient family systems.

This explains why in the Old Testament story of Esau and Jacob there was such a tremendous struggle over who was going to get the family blessing and birthright.  In that case, these two were twins; Esau had come out of the womb ahead of Jacob; that made him the eldest.  Therefore, by the custom of the time, most of the power and resources went to Esau, and Jacob was faced with having to circumvent tradition in very manipulative ways in order to get the role of leadership for which he was actually more gifted and capable.

I began my active ministry after seminary in a wonderful little Southern town in the middle of Tennessee.  One of the great things about living in such a place was hearing all the stories that comprised the heritage of the community.  One such tale was about the president of a bank whose two sons were the reverse of the prodigal and his elder brother.  In this case, the older son was a fun-loving rake, while the younger brother was a responsible, straight-arrow type, who always played by the rules.  When their father died, the two brothers found themselves alone in the funeral parlor with their father's corpse.

"You and I both know that money meant more to our father than anything else," said the older son.  "I think the most appropriate thing for us to do at this moment would be for each of us to put a thousand dollars in his hands and let it be buried with him. What more apt tribute could we pay to him?"

"Of course, that would be appropriate," responded

the straight-arrow brother.

The story has it that he went to the bank and got ten crisp one-hundred-dollar bills and put them carefully into his dead father's hand. Later that night, when nobody else was around, the older brother came, took the thousand dollars, wrote a check for two-thousand dollars and slipped it into his father's hand! The point is, if one had that kind of older brother in the first century, you'd be looking for somebody like Jesus to intervene and give you some help!

This is precisely the context in which Luke sets the Parable of the Rich Fool. An older brother was dragging his feet when it came to dividing the family inheritance; a younger sibling attempted to get Jesus involved in this process, since there was no court system in that day to handle such family conflicts. Interestingly enough, Jesus's response was curtly negative. He chose not to get sucked into this family fracas.

This is one of three occasions in the Gospels where someone asked Jesus to do something to a third party; in all three cases, he refused to reinforce such a manipulative way of dealing with problems. You remember the time when Martha was working busily in the kitchen while her sister Mary was sitting in the living room talking with Jesus (Luke 10:38-42). Martha got upset enough to demand that Jesus tell Mary that her place was in the kitchen helping with the meal. Jesus didn't go along with such a ploy.

He rather made the accuser deal with her own issues instead. Jesus never encouraged people to attempt to solve their problems by going behind the backs of others.

The other occasion was the day some men caught a woman in the very act of adultery (John 8:1-11). These individuals were very clear about what they thought the Law taught them to do in such situations. When they attempted to involve Jesus in the affair, you may remember that He refused to join them in their condemnation, turning the focus rather on their sins instead.

In the same fashion, here we find Jesus choosing not to deal with the complaint of the man in our story by siding with him against his brother. His approach was always to reinforce people's taking responsibility for their own actions and their own lives. We're never told to go to God and focus our attention on the offenses of others. When we go to God, we need to go with our own baggage, our own sack of rocks. We need to deal with the beam in our own eyes rather than the mote in someone else's eye. We best go to God as grateful people or as confessors, not as complainers or accusers.

There might have been, however, a deeper reason why Jesus refused to do what the man in our story asked of him. He might have sensed that the real issue here wasn't justice but a spirit of covetousness. It might have been in the man's body language or by his sheer anxiety to get the matter settled that Jesus perceived the real issue. At any rate, he responded by saying, "Take heed and beware of all covetousness, for a man's life does not consist in the abundance of his possessions."

Again and again in the Gospels, Jesus demonstrated a good nose for idolatry. He had more to say about the first commandment of Moses than all the other nine put together—"I am the Lord your God; you shall have no other Gods before Me." Jesus was very sensitive to our human tendency to elevate something that wasn't God into a godlike status. My hunch is that this is what Jesus detected behind this particular man's concern; so He proceeded to deal with him far differently from the way the man had expected.

You see, idolatry is no surface or incidental matter. It can lead to devastating consequence. Samuel Miller was the Dean of the Divinity School at Harvard University for many years. In one of his lectures, he tells of being in Munich in 1931, when German culture was flourishing. He went one night to the Bavarian National Opera House to see one of the last of what he called "The Metaphysical Clowns," a man named Karl Valentino. Charlie Chaplin would be a popular example of such a one, a person who dressed like a clown and did clownlike pantomimes, but actually was conveying profound truth through what he did.

The pantomime began with a stage that was bare except for one circle of light. The clown entered that circle and began to search very diligently for something he had lost. After a time, a policeman came up.

"Have you lost something?"

"The key to my house," replied the clown. "If I can't find it, I can't go home tonight."

With that, the policeman joined in the search with great intensity. Finally he asked, "Are you sure you lost it here?"

"Oh, no, I lost it over there," said the clown, pointing to a darkened part of the stage.

"Then why on earth are you looking here?"

"Because there's no light over there."

Such an exchange may seem terribly foolish on a superficial level, but beneath the action, Miller saw a profound symbol of human futility. To look for something where it doesn't exist is the ultimate formula for disappointment.

This is in truth what one always does in an act of idolatry. It's looking for an encounter with the Ultimate where ultimacy doesn't exist, and this can only result in failure. Jesus must have sensed that this was what the man was doing. By asking Jesus to help him get his inheritance, he was really thinking that the material sector of reality held in it all he needed to come to total fulfillment. Perhaps the real problem wasn't with the older brother at all, but with his confused understanding of reality itself. This is why Jesus told him to beware of all covetousness, adding, "The significance of one's life is never to be measured by the abundance of things that one possesses."

Let me underline that Jesus was never simplistic in the way he dealt with the material realm. Philosophically, there have always been economic absolutists on both ends of the continuum. There are people who say that the material realm is all there is, there being no other kind of reality except the realm of things. At the other extreme, there are those who say that wealth, in and of itself, is evil and that any kind of private property or possession is lethal to the human spirit.

Jesus, however, was never an oversimplifier; he didn't identify with either of these extremes. His attitude toward the material dimension of life seemed to be one of sanity and balance. He didn't take a vow of poverty, for example. Proof of this is the fact that he was often accused of being a glutton and a wine bibber, of loving the good things of life too much. He never said that simply possessing something is evil in itself. When he was arrested at the end of his life, he was wearing a seamless robe—a fine and valuable garment—and he numbered many wealthy individuals among his best friends. One of his heroes, the Good Samaritan, was obviously well-to-do and had resources out of which he was able to act redemptively.

I think Jesus would say that possessing private property can help individuals develop morally. Think about it. How can you ever become a responsible individual if you never have anything for which to be responsible? If you never let people experience ownership of any kind, all they will ever know is infantile dependency. There's no way to develop a sense of responsibility apart from having something for which you're responsible.

I was listening some time ago to a radio program dedicated to the memory of Martin Luther King, Jr. They replayed his great speech delivered at the Lincoln Memorial. Hearing it caused me to remember my struggles as a minister back during the sixties, when people used to say, "Let the black people become responsible, and then we will give them the right to vote." I'd always counter by asking, "How are they ever going to learn responsibility until we give them something for which they can be rightfully responsible." To say to a child, "Learn to read, and then I'll give you a book," or "Learn to swim, and then I'll let you go into the water," is a counsel of futility indeed! We have to have something that is our own in order to learn how to be responsible stewards.

I believe that Jesus understood this fact, which is why you don't find Him saying either that wealth was everything or wealth was evil. What Jesus did say quite clearly was that the material order can do certain things for us humans and that it can't do other things. It doesn't hold all of the resources that you and I need to be fulfilled as human beings. If we place any material object on the altar of ultimate importance, hoping to extract from it everything that feeds the hungers of our heart, we're going to be badly disappointed.

When I wrote earlier that Jesus had a good nose for idolatry, I meant He could sense when someone was expecting too much from a given reality and was quick to warn of such a mistake. This is what we see Him doing here with the man who was so upset about his inheritance. He was calling him to the realization that what a person has doesn't define what a person is.

Then Jesus said in effect, "This reminds Me of a story," and proceeded to hold up the picture of what is popularly known as the Parable of the Rich Fool. Let us look at it closely.

A wealthy farmer has a bumper crop one year. He thought to himself, "What shall I do, for I've nowhere to store all this grain? I know. I'll pull down my barns and build bigger ones, and then I can house all this grain and foodstuff. Then I'll say to my soul, 'Soul, you've ample goods laid up for many years; take your ease; eat, drink, and be merry.'" But God said to him, "You fool, this night your soul is required of you, and the things that you've prepared, whose will they be then?" Jesus concluded by saying, "So it is with the one who lays up riches for himself, and isn't rich toward God."

Notice, first, the adjective that God uses in this situation. He didn't label this one as good or bad, but rather "foolish." Here was a man who was already rich, a farmer whose land brought forth in one season such an abundant harvest that he had no shelter big enough to house the surplus. So he decided that he'd tear down what he had and make even greater provision to keep all the produce for himself. Having done that, he said confidently that now all his needs were met forever, that he didn't have to worry anymore, that he had provided for all eventualities; now he could take his ease—eat, drink and be merry, and forget about everything else.

It's precisely this kind of person that our culture would single out as a real success. But Jesus, a Galilean peasant who had virtually nothing to call His own, declared this way of living profoundly foolish.

Why do you think Jesus took such a position? I'd like to suggest three possible clues.

First of all, the man was described as foolish because no amount of material wealth can give human beings security against all the uncertainties of our life. To put it simply, things can take you only so far and can do only so much for you. We all have hungers and needs that no amount of wealth can touch. For example, money by itself can't make another person love you or stay with you or cherish you.

A few months ago I saw a rerun of that movie classic, *Citizen Kane.* One of the turning points occurred when the wife of the rich central figure announced that she had had enough and was going to leave him. He said, "But you can't," and she answered, "I am going to," and out she walked. There he was, in a magnificent estate surrounded by a whole cadre of servants. Yet for all that wealth and influence, he was powerless to make someone about whom he really cared remain by his side. You can't force another to love you with money alone, nor can you forestall the approach of death. You can't, no matter how much you have, empower yourself to live forever. There are certain things that material resources simply can't supply.

This is one of the points that Jesus was making in this story. He affirmed that our human hungers are of such a nature that there's only one Resource that possesses all that we need, and that Resource is the Holy One himself. If you build your hopes on anything other than the unfailing mercy of God, you'll eventually find yourself without what you need.

In another passage, Jesus spoke of building one's house upon sand or upon a rock (Matthew 7:24-27), and I invite you to think about the following possibilities in that light. Should a doctor say to you that you've only two months to live, or your spouse tells you that he or she is leaving, you're likely to find yourself crumbling if your life hasn't been built on God's foundation. The rich fool wasn't evil, mind you. There's no hint that he made his fortune dishonestly. He was foolish, however, to think that it could do for him what in fact it didn't have the power to do.

A second reason for describing this man as foolish is that he had missed the genuine delight that comes from an experience of profound gratitude, from realizing how much he had received that was utterly beyond his deserving. One of the highest joys lies in recognizing the primal Grace behind all things. This farmer's egotism and lack of gratitude are awesome, indeed. Notice how often the words "I," "my," and "mine" occur in this short story. Here's a man who obviously thought that his efforts were the only source of the great bounty he'd just harvested.

I heard once of an agronomist who used a computer to analyze all the components involved in the growing of a record wheat crop. His conclusion was that the universe provided about ninety-five percent of the energies, while the farmer accounted for about five percent. When you consider the mysteries of rain and soil and seed and sunshine and the part they play, then it's almost comical to hear the farmer in this story speaking of "I" and "mine" as if his efforts had been the only factor in this harvest. This is narcissism at its worst, and demonstrates how limited one's vision can be.

Kentucky, the state of my birth, is technically called "a commonwealth," and in that term is the profound recognition that all wealth is more of a social than an individual reality. No one of us can acquire wealth nor maintain wealth apart from what others have done for us. Think of those who taught us how to read, write, compute, and work. One of

the sterling joys of life is recognizing that we're playing just one part in a vast symphony of existence.
Behind all that we have lies a graciousness that can't
be measured but only celebrated and acknowledged
with genuine humility and gratitude.

A reason, then, why this particular man wasn't so
much evil or bad as tragically foolish, lies in the fact
that he thought more highly of himself and his part
in things than he ought to have thought. Also, he
thought too little of the grace and mystery that were
basic to his condition. There's food for delight in
simply being able to get up in the morning, in realizing that the world is still here, in having a measure of
health and seeing the sun come up, while the seasons
move about us in their mysterious procession.
There's much over which to be genuinely astonished
and for which to be immeasurably grateful, when
mystery is your native home. We each play one tiny
instrument in a magnificent symphony, led by the
Great Conductor who creates melodious music and
harmony when we follow his lead. Here's the occasion for real celebration! The rich fool in our parable
missed that point completely. His foolishness lay in
his superficiality, his egotism, his lack of awareness
and gratitude.

A third clue as to why the man was called "foolish"
is found in the absence of generosity in this man. I
never tire of contending that generosity is the most
basic of all the virtues. In the time before time, in
the world beyond the worlds, the Bible suggests that

God said, "This wonder of aliveness is too good to keep to Myself. I want others to get in on this ecstasy and to experience this wonder." This is the biblical answer to the question, "Why something and not nothing?" Creation is at bottom an act of generosity—God sharing the bounty of what he was and what he had, which is why the farmer in the parable is so out of touch with Ultimate Reality. He was foolish because he missed, by 180 degrees, what it means to be made in the image of God. He looked on his abundance and said the very opposite of what God said in the beginning. He proposed to keep it all to himself, and this is the surest way of all to miss what life is finally about. Just as there's a delight in recognizing how much you have that you don't deserve or create, so there's another kind of delight also, a kind of potency, that lies in seeing your generosity bless and energize other people. This quality, and no other, lies at the root of our being the kind of creatures that we were meant to be.

Imagine, for a moment, that a neutron bomb has been dropped where you are. This particular weapon is the ultimate dream of the materialist, for it destroys all human life, but leaves all material things intact. Imagine that one of those kinds of bombs has been dropped in your area and by some unexplainable grace, you alone have been left to survive. There isn't another human being anywhere around to prevent your taking possession of anything you want, for nobody else now lives in all the world.

Think of what that would be like! Any house that you want is yours to live in. Any car that you want to drive and any piece of jewelry you would like can be yours, for there's nobody to stand in your way of possessing anything your heart desires. Every material resource is at your disposal. Now, ask yourself if you could find joy in living in any house, or delight in driving any car, or exult in wearing any ring or owning any possession if there were no one else with whom to share these experiences? What would a luxurious house mean if you were always alone? What kind of joy would a car be if you had to make each journey in it by yourself? We're relational by nature and relational in our needs. It's a deep part of our essential humanity to be able to share what we are and what we have with someone else.

When God judged the man in our parable to be a fool, it mustn't have been with scorn but with infinite sadness, for he had missed what it means to be a human being. Perhaps the deepest sadness of this man was that as he grew older, he had no joyful memories of having given anything to his children, or wife, or friends, or neighbors, or anyone else. He couldn't reminisce about having brought delight to others by what he had given to them. What a form of impoverishment indeed!

Another facet of this same truth is that the clear differentiation between what one *is* and what one *has* gets acted out in the moment of death. We shall all be separated from the things we possess at that awesome juncture. To this man, who hoarded all he owned for himself, Jesus posed this haunting question, "When you die, who will then own all this to which you're so attached?" My friend, death is going to make generous givers of us all. Everything we have will pass on to others eventually. "There are no pockets in a shroud," says an old Arab proverb, and most assuredly no way to take anything with you. All of which comes down to this: If we're made in the image of Generosity and if we're going to be generous ultimately, why not get in on the joy of participating intentionally in what is the very essence of our being?

This foolish man, who held onto everything and got none of the satisfaction of being grateful and generous, wound up losing all that he valued without experiencing the joy that could have been his.

There's an old story of a man who dreamed one night that he had died and was given a chance to visit both the Underworld and then the realm of Heaven. In this dream, though, the one thing that death did to people was to stiffen their elbows. No one in either realm could bend their arms; they were forced to live with this kind of physical rigidity. In Hell, the dreamer saw terrible conflict and agitation; everyone had bread in both hands and were very hungry but, given the stiffness of their elbows, they couldn't get it to their mouths. Each one was concerned only for himself or herself, and the misery was unspeakable. The dreamer was then taken to

Heaven, where all the human beings had the same physical disability, only these folk had discovered a solution. Although they couldn't feed themselves with the stiffened elbows, they could feed each other!

Generosity—a willingness to give—was finally the difference between Heaven and Hell, and this resonates quite precisely with this parable that Jesus is still telling us.

# 9

## The Pharisee and the Publican

### *Luke 18:9-14*

*He also told this parable to some who trusted in themselves that they were righteous and despised others: "Two men went up to the temple to pray, one a Pharisee and the other a tax collector. The Pharisee stood and prayed thus with himself, 'God, I thank thee that I am not like other men, extortioners, unjust, adulterers, or even like this tax collector. I fast twice a week, I give tithes of all that I get.' But the tax collector, standing far off, would not even lift up his eyes to heaven, but beat his breast, saying, 'God, be merciful to me a sinner!' I tell you, this man went down to his house justified rather than the other; for everyone who exalts himself will be humbled, but he who humbles himself will be exalted."*

—

With the possible exception of the story of the Good Samaritan, where a despised social outcast is depicted as being morally superior to a priest and a Levite, no parable was more shocking than this account of a Pharisee and a tax collector going up to the temple to pray. The conclusion Jesus drew stood the conventional religious wisdom of that day on its

ear, and must have left the original hearers absolutely
aghast. Yet through it all broke clear a vision of the
Holy One that is of great importance. Let's look
with care at this short but startling story.

The main figures here were well-known entities in
Jesus's day. All of his hearers would have been familiar with individuals known as the Pharisees. They
were regarded in first-century Palestine as the most
devout religionists of the culture. Their name comes
from a root that means "pure." They sought for
purity in all things—in the way they observed the
Law, in their unswerving patriotism, in the care they
took to avoid all contacts with the impure. They
constituted a select and elite group who were the
very pillars of society and on the side of righteousness in every situation.

By the same token, all of Jesus's hearers also knew
what a tax collector was. Here was a class of individuals at the absolute opposite pole of the social strata.
No other occupation was more despised or looked
down upon. They were the unique creation of the
Roman way of doing business. Whenever a country
was conquered, the Romans recruited opportunistic
local citizens to collect revenues.

Obviously, it was a dirty business. Nobody likes
to pay taxes under any circumstances, but to have a
member of one's own nation and race go to work for
the occupation forces and also make a profit out of
such an enterprise was reprehensible. The individuals who stooped to this occupation were regarded as

traitors of the worst sort, as well as thieves and scoundrels. What the term *quisling* (Nazi collaborator) came to mean in World War II conveys the kind of scorn tax collectors received in first-century Palestine. They were the individuals for whom no decent human being had any respect or hope for future improvement.

The first element of surprise in the parable lies not in what the Pharisee did when he went up to the temple to pray, but in the fact that a tax collector would ever be found in such a place doing this sort of thing. Pharisees were famous for their religious enthusiasms, and the prayer that flowed from the lips of this one was vintage Pharisaic piety. "God, I thank thee that I am not like other men, extortionists, unjust, adulterous, or even like this tax collector. I fast twice a week, and I give tithes of all that I get."

A German scholar, Joachim Jeremias, has uncovered another first-century Pharisaic prayer that goes like this. "I thank Thee, O Lord, my God, that Thou hath given me my right with those who sit in the seat of learning and not with those who sit on the street corners. Why, I am early to work and they're early to work, but I am early to work on the words of the Torah, and they're early to work on things that are of no moment. I weary myself—they weary themselves, but I weary myself and profit thereby— they weary themselves to no profit at all. I run, they run, but I run toward the Age To Come, they run towards the Pit of Destruction."

The point is, Jesus wasn't unfairly depicting the Pharisees in this story. They were morally superior to most other human beings. They not only knew this, but also weren't hesitant to apprise other people of this fact as well. There was no secret to the pride they had in themselves or their disdain of others. This Pharisee's performance in the Temple involved no surprise at all.

There may have been mild surprise, however, over the actions of the other party in this drama. As a rule, tax collectors didn't frequent the Temple precincts or demonstrate the kind of contrition that Jesus depicts here. This particular one remained a far way off, not even lifting his eyes to Heaven, but beating his breast, the center of all decision making, saying simply, "God, be merciful to me, a sinner."

This wasn't ordinary, predictable behavior at that time, but whatever surprise may have been felt at that image is nothing compared to the earthquake of shock that must have followed Jesus's next statement. "I tell you this man that is the tax collector went down to his house justified, rather than the Pharisee. Everyone who exalts himself will be humbled, but he who humbles himself will be exalted."

When Jesus said those words, I'm confident a horrified gasp went up from all of the hearers. Talk about turning the world upside down—this was it! To suggest that the God of all righteousness, the Creator of the universe, the Author of the Ten Commandments would be more pleased with a traitorous scoundrel than a person of moral rectitude was absolutely staggering to what the Pharisees had taught all their lives. They probably couldn't believe their own ears. In effect, their conventional system of values was turned bottom side up!

This event reminds me of something I read several years ago around Halloween time. There was a large supermarket in New Jersey that had gone to a system of computer labeling. All the clerk had to do was run an item over a scanner that automatically records the price. Some juvenile pranksters, however, who knew a lot about computers broke into the store, and proceeded to change the prices on hundreds of items. They marked hams as selling for twenty-five cents, while a package of peas was going for twelve dollars. When the store opened the next morning and customers began to check out, total chaos emerged. They had to close the store in order to check all the prices on all the products. This disruption of the relationshipship between price and value is a modern parallel of the impact Jesus's parable must have made on the people who first heard it.

I want to pause and acknowledge that the shock those folk experienced that day grew out of genuine moral concern. A superficial reading of this parable could lead to ethical chaos. Was Jesus actually suggesting that it really didn't matter what people did with their lives, that one sort of behavior was no different from any other? Take this Pharisee, for example. If we can bracket for a moment the prejudices we've built up across the centuries to such persons, the way this man depicted himself represents real moral achievement. He says in all honesty, "I am not an extortioner, not unjust, not an adulterer." Let's face it, this is no mean accomplishment indeed, to order your business affairs along the lines of justice and honesty and your personal interactions along the lines of non-exploitative chastity.

Ask yourself, "If we didn't have people like this, how long could any society last? What permanence and stability would there be to any social fabric if there weren't many folk who chose to use their power in this way?" But that wasn't all. This Pharisee went on to report that he fasted twice a week and tithed everything he had. Helmut Thielicke, a wise German interpreter, says you can tell a person is serious about his or her religion when it affects two things: one's stomach and one's pocket book! We're all familiar with folk who turn to God when some crisis occurs. These are the people who become very religious when they get to the end of their ropes, like the sailors in Coleridge's *The Ancient Mariner* who cried: "To prayers—all is lost."

But it's something very different when you find human beings allowing their belief in God to affect the level of their bodily comfort. Fasting, you see, has never been a pleasant experience. It's somewhat akin to the discipline of becoming a marathon runner. These people don't just run when they feel like it. They assume a discipline they have to keep whether it feels good or not, adding more and more distance as time goes by. When people stay with such a regime for a long period, you realize they're serious about this endeavor. And individuals who engage in repeated periods of fasting for religious reasons are not to be written off lightly as uncommitted.

To fast twice a week is an extraordinary display of willpower, as is this other practice the Pharisee alluded to—the tithing of all the resources he came to possess. Money, after all, is one of the most basic forms of potency available to human beings. It enables us to do, and have, any number of things, which is why it's such an ally to our egotism. If I control a lot of money, that means I possess the ability of having my own way in a variety of forms. To take that pool of power and voluntarily relinquish control over part of it out of loyalty or affection for God is again a significant religious act. To take ten percent of all I have and give it to others is truly impressive.

Here was a person who was serious enough about God to let it affect both his stomach and his pocket book. For Jesus to suggest that this sort was religiously inferior to a man who had no spiritual track record at all, but in a moment of desperate crisis came begging for mercy is understandably upsetting. There's no indication in the parable that the tax collector intended to change his behavior or promised any reparation at all. He simply cried out for mercy in a time of need, which is religion of the most prim-

itive, self-centered kind. No wonder Jesus's hearers
were aghast.

Do the Ten Commandments correspond to anything real? Are they actually "laws" like the law of
gravity, descriptive of the way reality is put together,
things that can't be broken without consequences?
Or is all of this fantasy? How could a man who had
always been part of the problem and never part of
the solution finally turn out to be more in favor with
God than one who had taken morality seriously? We
need to acknowledge the revolutionary and even
threatening implications of Jesus's words here.

Helmut Thielicke warns that if we read this parable too superficially, the tax collector's humility could
become the norm instead of what is reflected in the
Pharisee's behavior. In fact, he composed a prayer
that could be said out of position. "I thank Thee,
God, that I am not as proud of myself as that
Pharisee. To be sure, I'm an extortioner. It's true,
I'm unjust and I am an adulterer, but that's what
human beings are, and that's the way I am and at
least I admit it. Therefore, because of my honesty, I
think I am a little bit better than that other one. I
commit fornication twice a week, I don't suppose
over ten percent of what I get comes from honest
work, but remember, I am being honest, God. I
don't kid myself. I've no illusions about myself.
Therefore, let your angels sing 'Alleluia' over a sinner
who is at least as honest as I am, willing to admit he's
a dirty dog, and not trying to hide behind some kind

of pretension like the Pharisee."

There's something quite upsetting, is there not, about making honesty and mediocrity into virtues, about saying in effect, "I don't live by any high moral code, but neither does anyone else, so at least I'm not a hypocrite." If you've worked in the church for very long and ever tried to get people involved in its affairs, you'll certainly have heard some people say, "Look, I'm not a perfect person, I don't claim to be, but at least I'm not a hypocrite like all those church-goers."

In the parish I served in Kentucky several years ago, there was a wonderful man, somewhat retarded in his mental development, but very devout and willing to serve the church in every way. During a visitation campaign one fall, this man volunteered to call on prospects for the church. We were a bit uncertain what to do, but finally sent him out with an experienced church worker.

That person came back giving a wonderful account. They had called on an individual who said heatedly, "I'm not going to go to church because it's nothing but a bunch of hypocrites," to which my slightly retarded friend replied, "Well, come on down, there's always room for one more." Seriously, though, there's something frightening about letting moral carelessness become the accepted norm. It's very important that we look more deeply at this parable and not conclude that the moral values in which our lives have always been steeped are of no consequence at all. I'm convinced that wasn't the point Jesus was making in this parable. What, then, does this story mean?

Now obviously, this Pharisee had reached a high level of moral maturity. He'd established control over his physical impulses and was the master of his money rather than his money being the master over him. In his journey from birth to the ideal, however, he had made a fatal mistake. He took his eyes off the goal at the end of the process, that completeness that is the high calling of God. He began to compare himself to the people alongside him rather than to the true Omega Point out ahead.

Two devastating effects followed this shift of focus. For one thing, he grew proud of himself and the level to which he had risen, and complacent about the distance he still had to grow toward the ultimate goal of maturity. Such a deflection of focus is lethal indeed to the process of vital growth. The Pharisee began to compare himself to someone in the second grade when he himself was in the tenth grade. This is what Jesus sensed as inferior in this particular man.

Can you imagine the Pharisee, having thus shifted his focus, coming out of the Temple with a desire to move further on and deeper into God's ultimate fullness? Of course not. Pride in himself and contempt for others had served to knock him completely off stride in the race he hadn't yet completed. The old question, "Compared to what?" is really crucial at this point. In any developmental endeavor, where you choose to fix your focus is all-important. The sidelong glance is very different from fixing your attention on the ultimate goal. When concentration of this sort is broken, the results are devastating.

Illustrations of this truth are all around us. If you follow any kind of sport very carefully, you know how important keeping your eye on the ball is. Again and again in football, someone fails to catch a pass. "He started to run before the ball got there," the commentator will say. "He didn't watch it all the way into his hands." This means he let something besides the ultimate goal deflect his attention.

Dr. Thielicke, whom I've quoted often, was the chaplain of the University of Hamburg during the terrible rise and fall of the Third Reich in Germany. At the end of the war he agonized with his fellow countrymen over all the chaos they had helped to bring on the whole world. He noted that had Germany stayed focused on the beam in their own eye, real moral renewal might have followed World War II. Somehow, however, the focus got shifted, and the Germans began to say, "But the British and the French and the Russians and the Dutch are not all perfect either." Before long, as a result of thinking this way the impulse to moral regeneration began to weaken. It happens every time we start looking around instead of ahead, for the energies to grow are kept alive by focussing on the ultimate goal.

I experienced this very same thing a few years ago when I made the transition from the Baptist ministry into the Episcopal priesthood. I attended the Episcopal Theological Seminary of the Southwest in Austin, Texas, to learn the many things about liturgy and church history and sacramental theology that were basic to competence in my newly chosen vocational niche. I threw myself into this year of "Anglicizing" with great energy. Late one afternoon, I was working away at my desk in the library when a classmate of mine in Liturgics 303 came by.

"You're really working late."

"I'm trying to finish this reading assignment for Liturgics class tomorrow," I replied.

"Don't you realize the teacher assigns more than anybody is expected to read? He means for you to use the next five years to get through all that material. Nobody else in the class is reading that much. You're overtaxing yourself unduly." With that, he walked on.

I pondered his words. I had assumed that assignments were assignments, that everybody was doing what the teacher prescribed. With that, I closed my book and went home to watch television. The next morning, in Liturgics class, we got to a point that was very important, something I wanted to know and needed to know. The teacher reminded us it was addressed in the assigned reading section for that day. No one in the class had read it. We were all caught off base, and it suddenly dawned on me that I had let what other people were doing deflect me from the goal that had brought me to the seminary in the first place. I wasn't there to conform to what other students were doing. I was there to learn all I could about something that was going to be essential to my future ministry, and I'd made the same mistake as this Pharisee and the football player and the German people. I'd substituted the sidelong glance for the clear focus on my ultimate goal, and this led me to thwart the impulse to grow.

This is what Jesus was criticizing in the Pharisee— not what he had achieved, but how he had taken his eye off the goal. On the other hand, the tax collector was in a very different position. He had achieved nothing really in terms of moral development. He was in kindergarten, you might say, in terms of what God wanted him to be, but something had happened in his life to jog him awake. Here he was honestly acknowledging his lack and crying out for grace to help in time of trouble.

We're not told by Jesus what it was that had brought that man to his senses and to his knees. However, let me pause and say that one of the ways that God's ingenious grace often works is to let us, in freedom, misuse our power and make an absolute mess of our own and others' lives. This usually entails a great deal of suffering under the impact of which, like the prodigal son, we sometimes come to ourselves and realize how far we are from the goal God originally intended for us.

I have seen this happen again and again and again. In a little country church that I served early in my career, there was a wonderful lady whose husband was a hardworking tenant farmer. Most of the time he was a respected citizen, a faithful husband, and a good father, but he had an erratic drinking problem. He could go for six months and be dry as a bone, and then something would snap inside. He'd go on a binge and spend all the family money, and become physically abusive to his wife and children.

I'd prayed for this man and talked to him directly about his situation many times, but somehow, the Gospel never seem to get through to him. Then late one Saturday night, I got a call to go to their house. When I got there, it turned out he'd been on his worst binge yet. Something his wife had said upset him, and he responded by beating her savagely.

But there was something about that event that brought him to his senses. He suddenly saw this person, who didn't deserve this kind of treatment, bleeding all around the face because of his violence. What he didn't want to be, came home so powerfully in that moment that he cried out. "I've got to have help. I want to be different. I must ask a Power into my life to change me." That was when he called for me. It was the beginning of a healing process. I got him to an Alcoholics Anonymous group in a nearby town. I got him in touch with some other people who know how to deal with that kind of sickness. He began to discover God's help in very tangible ways, and quickly began to move in a new direction.

In all likelihood, this tax collector had had a similar experience—some event that made him aware of how out of sync with his true self he really was. The very first of the famous Twelve Steps in AA is admitting that your life is out of control and that on your own you don't have the power to correct things. This is precisely what that tax collector was doing in the Temple. Jesus saw that while he was still at the kindergarten level in terms of achievement, he had at last assumed the stance that held the promise for growth. This occurs when a person honestly acknowledges the way it is, horrible as that may be, and accepts the fact that there's something bigger than he or she that is willing to help.

Our sins and lack of achievement are not the only realities on the stage of history. There is also God's everlasting mercy and unending patience, his desire, no matter what, to bring us to true completion. When grace of this sort gets access to our lives, as seems to be the case with this tax collector, then the possibility of growth becomes a reality.

I've already suggested that having prayed as he prayed, it would be hard to imagine the Pharisee leaving the Temple, saying "There are areas where I yet must grow and need God to help me." He'd taken his eyes off of the proper goal of human existence. It isn't hard, however, to conceive of the tax collector leaving the Temple in such a creative and hopeful frame of mind. He had broken through in his honesty to the one thing that is utterly essential to completion, and that is the availability of the divine grace that enables the whole process. By looking toward the goal and to God's grace, not at those alongside him, the one who was in kindergarten in terms of the past possessed more promise for the future than the proud, contemptuous tenth grader. This is why Jesus said the tax collector "went down to his house justified" more than the Pharisee. The attitudes expressed there spelled real difference when it came to future development.

In conclusion, then, let's underline what each of us can take away from this story for our own growth. Parables, remember, are about us, not about others. They're mirrors, finally, not portraits of other people.

First of all, the issue here is attitude, not achievement. Admittedly, the Pharisee was at a more advanced stage morally than the tax collector, but he'd stopped growing. He'd taken his eye off the ultimate goal God intended for him and started looking in directions that undercut his desire to progress. On the other hand, the tax collector has belatedly waked up to his real situation and was ready to begin to grow. In terms of the long future, this stance held more promise than the Pharisee's.

I'm sure Jesus was both glad and sad for each one of these men, but in opposite ways. He was glad for the Pharisee in terms of what he had accomplished, but sad that he had lost his focus and was now beginning to drift. On the other hand, he was sad for the tax collector's past and all the opportunities he had lost, but glad that he could at last see the light and was getting on with it. Given their present attitudes, the Pharisee had a past but no future, while the tax collector had the opposite—no past to brag about, but a genuine promise of a better future.

With God, the future is always more significant than the past. The Holy One is more interested in what we can become than in what we used to be. It isn't His nature to hold the past against us when we set out with Him to become new creatures. Jesus's point here is not one of moral relativity, as if it doesn't matter how we live or what we do. It's rather that our attitude toward God's goal and God's grace are the things that are most important.

My second point is that the criteria we select by which to evaluate our lives are equally crucial. "Compared to what?" is the basic question in any act of interpretation. Jesus is reminding us here that what other people are doing or failing to do is beside the point. God created us to participate in His kind of life and to experience fully His kind of joy. That is our true reason for being and the Omega Point toward which all moves. And the Good News is that the One who began such a sharing has the ability and the mercy and the patience to achieve this end. He promises, "You'll be perfect by My grace, if you'll only allow Me."

My third point is simply to note that what happened to the Pharisee is a special temptation to those persons who have achieved a high level of moral superiority. The people who have developed the capacity to fast and to tithe, who by hard and rigorous effort have made something significant of themselves, have a greater temptation to take their eyes off the goal. Someone has said that burnout is a major societal problem because it tends to affect the most conscientious and useful citizens in our culture. The wino down on an urban street corner isn't vulnerable to burnout. That will never be his particular nemesis. But the president of the Chamber of Commerce, the individual who is on six or eight boards, the person who really does want to be part of the answer and not part of the problem, there's the person who is susceptible to burnout.

In the same way, those who are really serious about their religion and want to become the kind of person that God wants them to be are the ones most in danger. They get halfway home, only to start looking around and seeing all the rascals and scalawags who are not doing half as much, and grow complacent. For such folk, it's doubly important to keep their eyes fixed on the goal and on the mercy that is the hope of the task being completed. Perfection, remember, comes as promise, not as some achievement we create on our own. We shall be full grown by God's grace, and no other way.

My last point is that we're not to judge others. If our reading of this parable has been correct—that we're to keep ourselves focused on the goal and on God's grace—then it isn't up to us to judge other people as to where they are, or how they're doing, or what is the level of their development. For one thing, this is an area where we simply don't have enough evidence on which to base a judgment. None of us ever knows enough about another to render an accurate verdict.

My wife and I were listening to a tape the other night on which a Roman Catholic priest asked some interesting questions. "Have any of you ever seen a motive? Do you really know all the reasons why a person does what that one does?" The answers, of course, are "No." We simply don't know what kind of things have happened and are happening in other people's lives.

I've a friend who's in a particularly angry stage of his life just now. He's in a church where there are lots of problems. He had a dream one night, during which Jesus came to him and spoke.

"Harry, I'm not pleased with your ministry these days. I've been listening to your sermons, and you sound more like the public prosecutor than the public defender. You're so judgmental and critical and harsh with your folk."

"But, Lord, I can't justify what some of my people are doing."

"Whoever asked you to justify them? That's my job. All I've asked you to do is to love those folk, forgive them, wash their feet, and nurture them."

My friend woke up and let the truth of that dream impact his life. He realized he'd gotten off the track of his true calling. "There and then," he later told me, "I shifted the focus of my ministry from the judge's bench to the basin and the towel. Instead of asking 'Where did you get your feet dirty, or why didn't you keep yourself more clean,' I resolved simply to deal with their dirt as Jesus dealt with mine." He now reports that the joy of being a minister has begun to return.

Remember, we never know enough about each other to judge. As we did not create them, so we are not ultimately responsible for them. That's God's job, and He's up to the task. It would be easy to look cynically at this tax collector and say, "I'll bet this is just another manipulative ploy, another con job," but we've no right to do that. God knows—of that we can be sure. To Him, "all hearts are open, all desires known; from Him no secrets are hid." We can trust that the One who saw deep into the heart of that tax collector that day saw a real desire to change and a willingness to receive the help to do it. And this is why Jesus shocked His hearers. "This man, scoundrel that he was, went down from the temple more in the favor of God than the man of vast moral achievements." God saw where the tax collector had his eyes fixed. The problem with the Pharisee was that God could never get his eye.

Martin Luther King, Jr., used to close many of his sermons with an old slave prayer, which went like this. "O God, I ain't what I ought to be, and I ain't what I'm gonna be, but by Your grace, I ain't what I used to be." Here's the insight that gives us hope.

There's a beyondness to which we yet aspire. We've fallen short of what we were meant to be; yet, there's Something bigger than our past or our sin, and that Something is the grace of God. If we keep our eyes fixed on that goal and that grace, we will, on the authority of God's promise, finally get home!

# 10

# The Great Banquet

## (Luke 14:15-24)

*When one of those who sat at table with Him heard this, he said to Him, "Blessed is he who shall eat bread in the kingdom of God!" But He said to him, "A man once gave a great banquet, and invited many; and at the time for the banquet he sent his servant to say to those who had been invited, 'Come; for all is now ready.' But they all alike began to make excuses. The first said to him, 'I have bought a field, and I must go out and see it; I pray you, have me excused.' And another said, 'I have bought five yoke of oxen, and I go to examine them; I pray you, have me excused.' And another said, 'I have married a wife, and therefore I cannot come.' So the servant came and reported this to his master. Then the householder in anger said to his servant, 'Go out quickly into the streets and lanes of the city, and bring in the poor and the maimed and the blind and the lame.' And the servant said, 'Sir, what you commanded has been done, and still there is room.' And the master said to the servant, 'Go out to the highways and hedges, and compel people to come in, that my house may be filled. For I tell you, none of those men who were invited shall taste my banquet.'"*

—

There are several motifs that occur again and again in Holy Scripture, and one of them is central to this particular story that Jesus told. All revolves around a party being given, generous hospitality being extended to a group of people, and then how they respond to such graciousness. This is actually the framework the Bible sets around the whole drama of history. So let us look carefully at these words and let them permeate our imagination and very lives.

I can think of no better image for the biblical understanding of God than that of a host or a gracious party giver. Paul Tillich claims he was launched on his philosophic quest as a fourteen-year-old when someone posed the question, "Why something and not nothing?" In other words, why does anything exist, or "stand out of nothingness," as the word *exist* literally means? If you allow Holy Scripture to be your resource here, the answer reverberates back. God is the link between nothingness and being, and not just any God, but a Generous One who wanted to take what He was and had and share this with others.

Don't you see, then, why Jesus's metaphor of a host giving a party is so apt? No image better gathers up the things that are revealed in Holy Scripture about God than this. Here's generosity, abundance, joyfulness and exuberance all bound up together. Medieval theologians used to make much of the doctrine that creation was finally, ultimately unnecessary, and this only adds intensity to this metaphor of host. The very best kind of parties are not given out of necessity or obligation. God knows, that's the reason behind many of them, but occasionally someone throws a bash for no other reason save that they love a good time and want to share with their friends. There's something authentically healthy about those things that come out of "the want to" side of personality. These realities are very different from what comes out of "the have to" side of things. The impulse to share what is good and not to keep it all to one's self is also a sign of personal soundness.

I lived out a big part of my young adulthood in Louisville, Kentucky, having gone to school there and then returning to serve a parish there for eleven years. About halfway into that experience, a friend said to me, "I've just discovered a country inn about thirty miles south of here near Brandenburg. It used to be an old stagecoach stop. Somebody has gone in, reclaimed the old building, and opened a restaurant called Doe Run Inn. I'd love to take you there someday. It's a secret that's too good to keep."

Not long after that, we did go. It was a nice trip out of the city and into the tranquil countryside. The inn was located in a beautiful valley with lots of shade trees. There was a stream running right beside it where you could still see the old mill wheel. There was a screened porch where you could sit and hear the water running. The food was excellent, and the atmosphere relaxing. It turned out to be an absolutely perfect way to spend an evening.

You can anticipate my response to all this. Hardly a week went by before I found myself doing exactly what my friend had done. I was telling someone else about Doe Run Inn and arranging to take them there. Across the next years, I estimate I've taken sixty or seventy people to that lovely old place. And the people I've taken have introduced the place to others. The point is, there's something about goodness that makes you want to share it.

This is precisely how the Bible accounts for everything coming to be. The Mystery behind it all isn't only the Holy One; that is, transcendent and in a category all by Himself. The Holy One is also the Generous One, and one way of describing creation is to see it as the party God has chosen to throw so that we could get in on some of His bounty and begin to know the joy of being party givers ourselves.

So, our parable begins on a familiar note. A host who had a house and food and all kinds of abundance wanted to share this with others, but then things took an unexpected turn. The generosity of the party giver wasn't met by gratitude or a positive willingness to respond. Amazingly, those who had received engraved invitations began to snub the host. When he sent his car around to pick them up, so to speak, they began to make all kinds of excuses and wound up refusing to attend at all.

Here's yet another parallel to the biblical story, for you don't get past the second chapter of Genesis before it becomes clear that what God wanted for creation and what occurred were not the same thing at all. Soon into the biblical story, the shadow of evil falls straight across the bright intention of the Creator. "Where did this evil come from," one has to wonder and, "Why was it allowed to exist in the first place?"

To put the issue quite bluntly, if God is all-powerful and all-good, as the Bible seems to imply, why is there so much in God's creation that is so painful and destructive? Couldn't that kind of Being have structured things somehow to prevent all this that is so clearly at odds with the reality of joy? It's the question that believing people have to face, just as the reality of good is the issue for those who have no faith and claim to be atheists. They're called on to account for the problem of so much beauty and purpose on the premise of there being no God. But the believer's dilemma centers on the presence of evil.

No issue has invoked more debate across the centuries than this one. For example, a recent popular treatment of the subject is Rabbi Harold Kushner's book *When Bad Things Happen to Good People.* He takes the approach that many have adopted; namely, that you have to alter the ancient concept of God to account for evil. He says of the three assertions— God is all-powerful, God is all-good, and evil exists—only two can be embraced simultaneously, not all three. This means you can say that evil is real and God is all-powerful, but He can't be all-good, or else He'd use His power to eliminate evil. If God could put an end to evil and doesn't, this casts a shadow on His goodness. Or you could say that God is all-good and evil exists, so there must be a deficiency in God's power. If He really wants to eliminate evil but can't, one can no longer support the claim that God is omnipotent.

A third alternative is to do what the Christian Scientists do, which is to say that evil doesn't really exist, but is only an illusion. This leaves the two affirmations about God intact, but in a world that has witnessed the Holocaust, it's hard to be realistic and say all this violence is merely in our minds and imagination.

Kushner himself opts for the first combination. He concludes the problem lies in God's power—that God, like us, is up against what he calls a random-ness in the world that even He can't master. This is actually how a great many serious thinkers have resolved this dilemma. They conclude evil exists because God is lacking in power. Woody Allen puts it this way: "I am not saying there's no God. I am simply saying that if One does exist, he is an under-achiever!"

I don't claim that I can resolve the mystery of evil better than all these other thinkers, but through my own intellectual struggles, I've come to a different conclusion than what I've just described. Let us go back for a moment and recall God's reason for creat-ing in the first place. I've been contending all through this book that God's only intention in creating was to share His own special kind of joy. The wonder of His aliveness was regarded as too good to keep to Himself. God wanted others to get in on the ecstasy He was experiencing in being who He was and doing what He did. There was no emptiness in God that needed to be filled. There was rather a bottomless fullness he wanted to share. This, then, is the final intention, and it raises the question, "What would have to happen for this goal to be attained? What would God have to do to make this desire a reality?"

As I break down that question, I discern three ingredients, if you will, of such an enterprise. To be able to participate in God's kind of joy, human creatures would have to be given a measure of power, the ability to make things happen. They'd also need to posses a measure of freedom. The divine Being isn't some mechanical robot, but a living Spirit who freely chooses to create and then freely takes delight in what He's done. The third ingredient would need to be a special spirit of wisdom that knew how to use power in ways that brought delight to Himself and blessing to all who were affected by these actions. To act is to make a difference, to alter the situation into which power is asserted. The secret of God's unique quality of spirit is that the difference God made wasn't just pleasing to Him or to others, but pleasing to both simultaneously.

This, it seems to me, represents the necessary

structure for God's joy to be shared. Not even an omnipotent God could have created the possibility for joy in any other way, which underlines the fact that the risk of failure was inherent in the goal God wanted to achieve. God could have withheld either power or freedom, and evil could never have been, but the joy would have been impossible as well.

What I'm saying is that this really is the best of all possible worlds, given what God wanted to accomplish. The fact that evil resulted isn't because there's some flaw in God's power or goodness. It roots back to the freedom that had to be given to make joy possible. It wouldn't have been true freedom if it couldn't have been used negatively as well as positively.

If you take the biblical stories seriously, the root of evil lies in the spirit possessed by the first human beings. In the Genesis account, the serpent challenged the idea that God was totally good. "He isn't One who always acts to bless those He touches," the serpent inferred. "He is at heart a Tyrant, an Exploiter, One who is holding you down to build Himself up."

In other words, the serpent accused God of thinking only of His own delight, not of those affected by Him, and encouraged the human to do the same thing. Whenever you pull asunder what seems to be joined together in God—personal delight and the will to bless—some form of evil results; the serpent's allegations against God prompted the humans to do just that. They forgot all about blessing the others, and in panic decided only to look out for themselves alone. This meant they stopped using their power to do both of the things God did, and the result was the unmaking of God's creation. The Holy One started with nothing and moved through chaos to order and beauty. Once His way of acting was rejected, and only "what is good for number one" shaped behavior, the reversal of that process began; order and beauty were turned back into chaos and finally into nothingness itself.

Why did this happen? I repeat, it isn't because there's a flaw in the design. If God's kind of joy is to be realized, there had to be power and freedom and a certain kind of spirit. That spirit got distorted, so the whole thing began to unravel.

"Evil" really is "live" spelled backwards, and it grows out of the very possibilities that had to exist for joy to be. Thus, instead of blaming God for evil and saying He is lacking in either power or goodness, I think we need to realize that it is we humans who have taken what God gave us and chosen to misuse it. The problem isn't that God has insufficient power, but rather that no amount of power could create the reality of joy coercively. What God is and wants for us is finally something highly personal. When you enter that realm, sheer brute strength can only go so far.

I remember when my son was about to have his sixth birthday. We wanted this to be a special milestone for him, so we bought presents we thought he most wanted and invited his best friends over for a great celebration. For some reason, however, he got up on the wrong side of the bed that morning, and nothing that whole day long turned out to suit him. He hated our presents and sulked through the whole party. I forced him physically to be present there, but there was no power in the world that could make him enjoy that occasion. Joy is finally something a human being has to experience willingly, and not even an all-good, all-powerful God can force that reality on another free spirit.

Going back to our parable, then, the host did all he could do in setting the stage for an experience of joy. What he didn't have the power to do was coerce his guests either to come or enjoy what was there once they arrived. They were the only ones who could complete the process, so to speak. Why they didn't do so? Why do humans who were made for joy in the first place choose to turn away in misery? There's no logical explanation for such self-destructive behavior. The Bible speaks of "the mystery of iniquity." That's what evil is ultimately—a deep and dark mystery. Why it happens, we can't finally say. That it happens and that we ourselves participate in it, who can deny?

But what happened when the desire of the party giver was thwarted? His first reaction was one of anger. Can you blame him? People are very uncomfortable with the image of the wrath of God. They say it doesn't square with a God of love and mercy and joyfulness. But wait, think again about the true nature of love. The opposite of this reality isn't anger but indifference. We never get angry about something that is unimportant to us. There's always an element of value involved in an outburst of anger, for something that truly matters has been violated. For the host to have shown no feeling at being rejected would have revealed that he didn't care in the first place; that would be inconsistent with the nature of authentic love.

The wrath of God, then, isn't the Almighty having an immature temper tantrum because he can't have his way. It grows out of deep frustration and sadness that what He wanted to give in terms of blessing isn't being allowed to happen. The wrath of God is simply an aspect of the love of God, a sign of how deeply God cares and wants to bless.

The host's second response, however, wasn't to give up on the idea of a party alogether, but to widen the invitation list. He sent out his servants to get the poor, the lame, the people who had massive physical problems. When this didn't fill up the hall, he sent out into countryside, into "the highways and the hedges," and invited the most socially unsophisticated of all the people in the community, those who'd never dreamed of ever being in the manor house.

This facet of the story, of course, had a historical dimension to it, similar to Jesus's story about the petulant children. He was defending Himself and explaining why He'd done what He did in His ministry. He'd been roundly criticized because He ate with sinners. It had offended the religious establishment that He'd reached out so deliberately to the social outcast. He was constantly being judged for the kind of company He kept. One of the things that He was doing here was holding up a mirror so those who criticized Him could see themselves.

The Jewish people were the very first ones who had been invited by this blessing God to come and enjoy His bounty. The Holy One said to Abraham, "I want to bless you and through you all the families of the earth." One of the objectives in giving the party was God's desire that the party goers would get into the spirit of it. Had that happened, God's spirit of joy would've spread.

Of course, the initial group of Jews didn't so respond, but that didn't quench the sharing impulses of God anymore than the establishment's rejection of Jesus discouraged Him. His turning to the tax collectors and sinners is of one piece with God's tenacious mercy. This story simply gives powerful expression to the deepest dimension of the Gospel. While there's nothing we can do to make God love us any more than He already does, neither is there anything we can do to make God stop loving us. There's both a stubbornness and an ingenuity in God's way of loving. He doesn't take away our freedom or shield us from the consequences of our evil, but often through those very traumas, God brings us to a new awareness.

In the Parable of the Prodigal Son, some people are shocked that the father would give the young son his inheritance when his spirit was so rebellious and his immaturity so great. Wasn't it folly to hand over matches to one who knew so little about fire? Yet, this is precisely how God's wisdom often works in relation to our freedom. He allows us to learn for ourselves through pain what we refuse to be taught from those wiser than we; in the prodigal's case, it worked. In the far country, he was dumb enough to lose all that his father had been smart enough to make and save. He finally wound up in the lowest place a Jewish boy could go, having to feed pigs, of all things! He collided head-on with all his faulty notions of himself and the world and his father, and there in the pit of failure, Jesus said, "He came to himself." The term is a medical one for waking up from a coma, and it marked the turning point in his process of maturing.

This is very reassuring to the parents of teenagers who seemingly refuse to listen to anything they're being taught. Even in the midst of headlong rebellion and self-destructive behavior, God isn't absent or without resources to bless. Self-imposed pain is oftentimes a great teacher, which explains why neither God nor Jesus had abandoned hope for the lowliest of the outcasts. These folk were often the most ripe for coming to themselves precisely because of what their mistakes had taught them.

God is far more interested in a person's future than in that one's past. He is more concerned for what we've learned from our mistakes than the fact that we've made them. Notice carefully that when the prodigal did venture back home, he encountered nothing but gladness and acceptance from his father. His father doesn't say a word about all the inheritance the prodigal had lost. The important thing was what he'd learned, not what it had cost.

Here's the wonderful reminder that it's never too late to turn back to the merciful Father. Once a child, always a child. We didn't create our relationship with God by what we did; therefore, we can't forfeit or destroy that relationship by what we do or fail to do. The bond between us is His gift to us. Letting our sin teach us what we need to learn is part of the way that God's mercy works. My hunch is that the people who were invited last were not only the most ready but the most astonished of all. They realized they had wasted their substance and been arrogant and unwise; out there in the darkness they might have assumed that their badness was bigger than anything else, that they'd forfeited forever the chance to sit at the table and get a glimpse of the party giver's face. And the wonder of what the prodigal discovered was the wonder that broke over these individuals as well. They were still included in spite of all they had done! Lo and behold, God's goodness was bigger than their badness, and those who knew best how little they deserved it, for that very reason, appreciated it the most.

The last thing that I want to say about this story, however, is the note of warning that is inherent here. Mark it down; with all His heart, God wants us to come to the party of His joy, but at the same time, it is possible to miss out on it altogether. The reason isn't that creation is flawed, but that you and I are ultimately free. We're the only ones who can sense that God's spirit of delighting and blessing is the essence of reality, who can decide to embrace that and begin to embody it.

You see, we can miss the party by being arrogant and destructive in the way we use our power, or we can miss it by being so caught up in everyday routine that we confuse the good for the best and never really get around to being what we could be.

What I am trying to suggest is that there are ways to miss the party that aren't blatantly evil. If you'll look at the three excuses that were made in the parable, two of them had to do with work and the other had to do with family. These people confused the good for the best, and settled for living at a level far below the joy God wanted for them.

The final warning is that I can miss the place that has been prepared for me from the foundations of the earth by absolutely defying God's design of creation and living in total opposition to His way of love, or I can drift into such mediocrity that the high purpose of God is lost by neglect. I can miss the kingdom by being so caught up in my own routines that I fail by default.

A Lutheran minister wrote a homily once on this parable and I want to close this chapter by quoting it. The first time I experienced it, I was startled at the way it became parable for me in terms of what it enabled me to see. My hope is it will do its redemptive work in you as well.

*Herman closed the front door gently, took off his coat, and hung it in the closet. He unzipped his overshoes, first one and then the other, slid them off, and bent down to put them in the closet. There a wild jumble of boots and rubbers confronted him. Muttering under his breath, he began to sort them out and started arranging them two by two. Then he carefully placed in his own side by side in the last square inch of space, and then he closed the door gently. It wouldn't close. A parka jammed in hurriedly was blocking the door. Herman methodically rearranged the coats and jackets and sweaters. Then he closed the door gently.*

*For one flashing second he thought, "Why didn't I just slam that door? Why didn't I just throw my overshoes in on top of the heap like everybody else does? Why do I always choose to close doors so gently?" But it was only a momentary spasm. "One just doesn't do things that way," he said to himself.*

*The house was strangely quiet. The cat meowed plaintively and rubbed against his leg. He stooped over and patted her.*

*"Hello, Mrs. Beasley."*

*Funny name for a cat, but Tammy had insisted on*

*calling her Mrs. Beasley after she'd seen a television doll commercial. A ridiculous name for a cat really.*

"I wanted to call her Whiskers or Tabby, but Tammy insisted on Mrs. Beasley." Herman smiled to himself. "Mrs. Beasley."

The cat followed him to the refrigerator. He poured some milk into her dish and opened a new can of cat food.

"Where is everybody?" he asked the cat as he spooned out food into her dish. Then Herman closed the refrigerator door gently.

"Last minute shopping, I guess."

He mused about it as he went upstairs to take off his clothes.

"Lorraine is always shopping at the last minute. Well, not always, but a good bit of the time. Probably wieners and beans for dinner tonight."

He was mildly irritated. The bedroom was a shambles. Lorraine's slacks and blouse were thrown on the bed. The closet doors were flung open. A dress hung askew on a crooked hanger. Her shoes had obviously been quickly rummaged through. He sighed and opened the closet door gently. He hung his suit away, carried his shirt to the clothes hamper in the bathroom. He had to push Tammy's sneakers off the mat as he hung up her towel. He scooped up her play clothes, crammed them together with his shirt into the hamper.

"Life would be so much easier if people would just take a little time to be more tidy. It would make my job easier too," he thought, as he ran water into the sink.

He had to plan his day—this was Herman's way. It was the only way he could manage to retain any semblance of sanity, and then inevitably somebody came along and disrupted his plans. Suddenly a great weariness came over him. He leaned on his hands in the water, random thoughts begin to flicker through his mind like fragments of a ragged film running through a broken projector. Would the company expand or relocate? Maybe we will have to move. Jennings would sure like my job—he's a manipulator. The house needs painting. The living room rug is pretty worn. Has the washing machine been repaired?. Wonder how much it was? Tammy's tooth is loose; maybe it will drop out. Jennings has just built a new house—his payments must be very steep. No wonder he wants my job. At least Lorraine sews her own clothes; that's a help. We've got to throw a party soon—there are lots of invitations to pay back. Oh, the pledge card from the church, it has just come. Got to get the car winterized; should have it sanded and painted if I am going to drive it another year. I wonder if we will get any tax breaks this year? Didn't get anything done today like I planned. That dumb Jennings—he messed up my whole afternoon— had to drop everything and go to a special session to consider his hair-brained plans—he seems to think he is the only idea man in the company. How do they expect me to get my work done with all these interruptions?

He dressed and closed the door gently. He picked up Lorraine's slacks and blouse and hung them away. Poor girl! I know she gets fed up with her daily routines.

*Breakfast, cleaning, getting Tammy off to kindergarten, cooking, washing, ironing. I know she'd like to get out. At least I see grown people every day. This house must be like a prison to her. He closed her closet door gently, and went downstairs. Mrs. Beasley rubbed his leg and he picked her up.*

*"Six o'clock—wherever could they be?"*

*Then he started to sort through the mail, and it was then he saw the note.*

*"Herman, we waited until almost five for you and then just had to leave. Please get a cab and join us. You missed Tammy's birthday party last year. Try not to miss it again this year. Lorraine!"*

*Tammy's birthday party. At a restaurant that caters such things. They had planned it; he'd been a little reluctant at first, but okay, the sixth birthday is a milestone, and he could see Tammy that very morning saying, "Daddy, you'll be there, won't you?" and he'd given her a big hug.*

*He looked at the clock, and it said 6:15, and somewhere in his soul, Herman heard a door slam shut. The kingdom of Heaven, so it's said, is like the time a man received an invitation—even conscientious Hermans can miss it because they confuse the good and the best.*

—

We've been invited, brothers and sisters. Don't let anything cause you to overlook or forget that!

# About the Author

JOHN CLAYPOOL, IV, was born in Kentucky, reared in Tennessee, and now lives in Birmingham, Alabama with his wife Ann; they are the parents of three grown children.

He graduated from Princeton Theological Seminary, Southwestern Baptist Theological Seminary (Fort Worth), and Episcopal Theological Seminary of the Southwest (Austin, Texas). He is rector of Saint Luke's Episcopal Church, Birmingham, Alabama.

He is also the author of *Tracks of a Fellow Struggler* (1974), *The Preaching Event* (1980), and *Glad Reunion* (1985). *Stories Jesus Still Tells* is his seventh book.